DIARMUID GAVIN
DESIGN
YOUR
GARDEN

DIARMUID GAVIN
DESIGN
YOUR GARDEN

Contents

 LONDON, NEW YORK, MUNICH, MELBOURNE AND DELHI

First American Edition, 2004

Published in the United States by
DK Publishing, Inc., 375 Hudson Street,
New York, New York 10014

04 05 06 07 08 10 9 8 7 6 5 4 3 2 1

ISBN 0-7566-0373-0

Copyright © 2004 Dorling Kindersley Limited
Text copyright © 2004 Diarmuid Gavin

A Cataloging-in-Publication record for this book is available from
the Library of Congress.

Discover more at **www.dk.com**

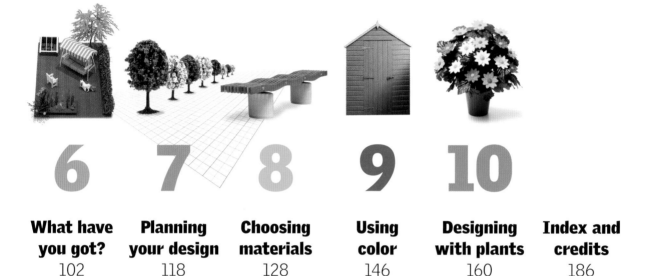

Project editor	Zia Allaway	**Picture research**	Melanie Watson
Project art editor	Colin Walton	**Illustrations**	Richard Lee
Editors	Vicky Willan,	**Media resources**	Lucy Claxton
	Christine Dyer	**DTP designer**	Louise Waller
Art editor	Clive Hayball	**Production controller**	Heather Hughes
Senior managing editor	Anna Kruger	**Color reproduction**	in the UK by MDP
Senior managing art editor	Lee Griffiths	**Printed and bound**	in the UK by Butler and Tanner

Foreword Planning and designing a garden doesn't have to be difficult. It's all about the process, having a set of guidelines, and the **confidence and knowledge** to follow them through. For some people, creating their own perfect garden is instinctive: they know what they want and have a good idea of how to achieve it. But for many, designing gardens is a mystery. There are so **many different disciplines involved** in defining and laying out a yard that it's easy to lose your way, especially in this day and age when we have so much choice. Books, magazines, and television programs bombard us with images of gardens, ranging from the very simple to the hugely aspirational, bogging us down in a quagmire of information and ideas, while we try to define what's right for us.

In *Design Your Garden* **I aim to dispel some of the mystery** and set out in 10 simple steps the process involved in creating your ideal yard. Whether you've bought a new house with a blank canvas, an older property with a garden that's had previous lives, or you just want to improve what you already have—I will help you to measure up and analyze what you've got, before **harnessing your imagination** to create something beautiful, productive, and coherent. Be inspired by the gardens of wonderful designers from around the world, and focus on what you want to achieve. The ability to fulfill your dreams is within these pages, to **design a unique outdoor space** that will give you joy for a long time to come.

Diarmuid Gavin

To Nik Linnen

Obrigado!

6

1
What do you want?

When designing your garden, start by asking yourself, "What do I want?". It seems obvious, yet **it's easy to forget to focus** and, instead, be blinded by what you've got—a square yard, shed, pond—but this will never lead you to plan your dream garden.

The first thing I do when taking a brief from clients is to **bombard them with questions** about themselves. Do they live alone, with a partner, or do they have a family? How old are the kids? Do they have pets? Do they like to party or prefer quiet meals with friends? Gradually, a picture of their lifestyle begins to emerge and I start to understand what makes them tick. It's only at this point that I can begin the design process for their outdoor space.

For your garden, ask yourself the same questions. Buy a notebook and jot down everything you love. **Your idea of heaven** could be an outdoor dining room edged with fragrant flowers, or a jungle of lush foliage set around a tranquil pool. Include on your list things that make you happy: dancing till dawn, cafés in Paris, **walks in the park**, lying on a sun-drenched beach, quiet nights at home by an open fire—whatever makes you feel good. Then ask the other members of your household to do the same, and combine your lists. Don't be hampered by what you know is going to be possible, and pretend you have the **luxury of a limitless budget**, an ideal site, and perfect climate. You may have to temper your ideas later on, but at least you'll have the essence of your dream outdoor space.

Once you have what you want, make a list of **what you need**. Take time to compile this, and make sure you miss nothing. It can be difficult—and more expensive—to include sheds or a place for the garbage cans once the plan is finished and building work complete, so make sure everything you need in your garden is listed before you start drawing.

Buy a notebook and jot down everything you love...then ask the other members of your household to do the same and combine your lists

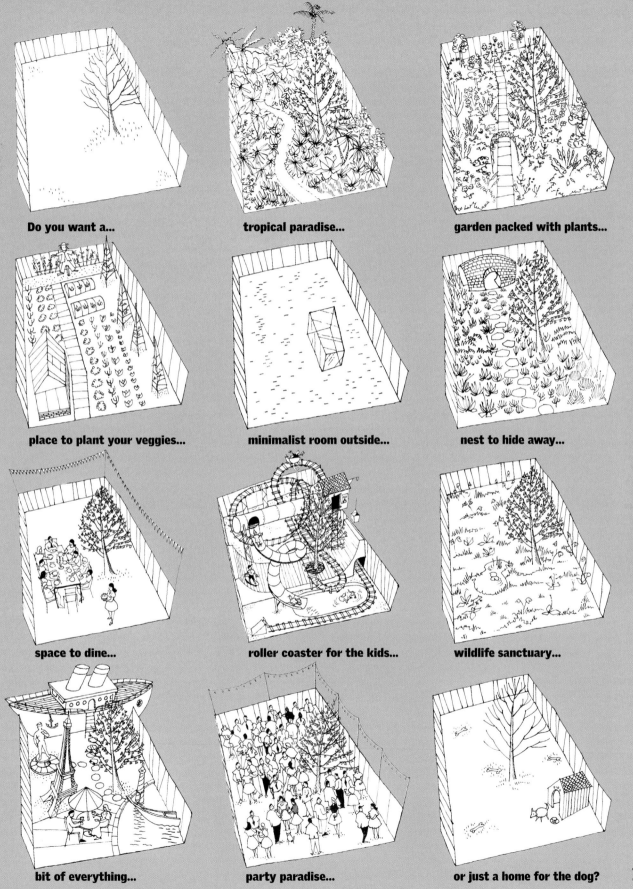

Do you want a...

tropical paradise...

garden packed with plants...

place to plant your veggies...

minimalist room outside...

nest to hide away...

space to dine...

roller coaster for the kids...

wildlife sanctuary...

bit of everything...

party paradise...

or just a home for the dog?

11

Space to dine

An area for table and chairs will definitely increase your enjoyment and use of the garden. The most obvious site for an outdoor dining room is close to the house, with easy access to the kitchen, but if your garden faces north, you may find a sunny spot at the end of the yard more comfortable. A setting among plants or by water evokes a relaxed, romantic ambience, while a covered patio offers shelter from the elements, extending its usefulness.

Room to play

Gardens are fun places for children and grownups to play. Trampolines, popular for both kids and adults, are good for a laugh and keep you in shape, while more traditional wooden play equipment and treehouses suit informal designs. Gardens also make great places for parties. Use dramatic lighting to transform your space into a stylish nightclub as the sun sets.

A haven for flowers...

Borders bursting with flowers
define a garden for many people.
Creating a flower garden is an art
form, and the best designers show a
keen eye for color and shape. I love
these types of gardens because they're
constantly changing, not only with
the seasons, but day to day, and even
hour by hour, as light and shade fall
on petals and foliage.

and for food

Growing your own fruit and veggies is really rewarding, and lots of people are now using their gardens for organic produce. If you don't want to sacrifice all your flowers, why not plant a potager, and mix your blooms with lettuce and carrots? You'll find specialist nurseries offer a good range of unusual crops that aren't available in your local supermarket.

Secret retreats

A place to hide away and abandon your worries is a seductive idea. Modern lifestyles leave little time to relax, but gardens offer a refuge. Create a nest camouflaged by plants where you can re-energize and unwind. A treehouse or garden room may offer the perfect retreat, though a simple pergola seat in a secluded spot can also provide a sanctuary.

2
What's your style?

Everyone has an individual style. It influences the way we present ourselves to the world, and affects the clothes we buy, the makeup we choose, the car we drive, and how we decorate our homes. **Our choices say something about us**, who we are and what we aspire to be. The same is true of our outdoor space. Our style of garden reflects what we enjoy, and, if it is to the front of the house, it also gives a first impression to the outside world. But **style is not just about decoration**. It should be followed through with good design, and not just hint at your preferences, but present them in a clear, concise way.

Many garden styles we recognize today have evolved over hundreds, if not thousands, of years. They are often grand ideas that have been diluted and absorbed into smaller gardens, with various degrees of success. The best designs show a real understanding of another time and place, **capturing the essence of a style**, rather than creating a pastiche.

So, developing some knowledge about your chosen style is a starting point. It's also important to consider whether it's right for your yard; good design often means tailoring a style to suit what you have. But that doesn't mean you can't be quirky and amusing. There's no reason why you can't **create your very own version of Versailles** around your three-bedroom suburban castle. Style is just about doing something well.

To choose a style that's right for you and your yard, collect ideas from garden visits, magazines, and television programs, and jot down those that appeal to you. You could also look at different national styles—Japanese, Italian, French, and so on—and styles you like in other areas of life, and see if you can create a garden version of these.

On a more general level, ask yourself whether **you want a formal look**—a stately, refined garden based on symmetrical patterns and order, with straight lines controlling the yard—or an **informal design**, which revolves around curved shapes and relaxed lines that lead you through the garden. Examples of these styles are everywhere. Your task as designer of your yard is to look at as many as possible and consider how they might suit you. Even if you see a style that you don't like, try to work out what it is about the garden that doesn't appeal to you, because this gives you knowledge of **what will work for you**.

Contemporary style

This is probably the most misunderstood of all garden styles. Ask people what they think makes a garden contemporary and they will generally say that it should be uncluttered and minimal, with clean lines and exotic-looking plantings. But for me, the true meaning of a contemporary design is one that reflects the times we live in.

To be contemporary is to be "of the moment," influenced by what surrounds us now, whether it is developments in hard landscaping materials, building methods, architecture, engineering or the visual arts—including fashion, and graphic and product design.

Along with developments and trends in these areas, there are also fashions in contemporary planting styles, such as prairie plantings (*see pp168-9*) and planting with grasses. Materials in vogue in the garden include stainless steel, glass, concrete, western red cedar, Portland stone, and slate. These are all commonly used inside our homes, and people are now becoming more aware of their potential uses outdoors.

Contemporary gardens are also beginning to reflect current lifestyles. People want to spend more time enjoying their outdoor space, using it as an extended living room rather than just a place for plants. Stylish accessories, such as lighting systems and patio heaters, are important designers' tools, extending the time we can spend in our outdoor rooms. Gardens attached to new

To be contemporary is to be of the moment, influenced by what surrounds us now

Light fantastic *(opposite)* *Andy Sturgeon's "Situations" design for Westonbirt International Festival of Gardens 2003 used Ambidex steel walkways turned on their sides and filled with stones. Blue Perspex squares introduced color into these rock-and-metal walls.*

Inside out *(above)* *Young Dutch designer Paul Weijers blurs the lines between inside and out in this garden in Aalsmeer, Netherlands.*

Along simple lines *(right)* *Straight-edged geometric forms combined with minimal plantings—including giant horsetails, papyrus, and a Japanese maple—create this clean-looking garden. Designed by Andrea Cochrane, the concept for this garden in San Francisco reflects the Asian antecedents of the owners.*

25

Naturally sculpted (*left*) *Plants become sculptural elements in Jinny Blom's garden and landscape designs. Although she often groups them as they would appear in the wild, they are set out more formally in this space.*

Spatially aware (*below*) *In this Dutch garden, designer Jan Nickman has created a restful atmosphere using mostly natural materials. Large, geometric shapes set on diagonals open up and extend the space.*

homes are sometimes small, and designs must suit these compact spaces. Water features, such as wall and bubble fountains, are useful for small yards, patios, and courtyard gardens, and offer sound, movement, and dramatic focal points.

Garden evolution The evolution of the contemporary garden began in the 1950s. Earlier in the century, gardens were dominated by Victorian bedding plans or imitated Gertrude Jekyll–style cottage borders. Then, after World War II, a huge rise in home ownership meant that ordinary people suddenly had their own yards, and a newfound freedom to explore the world of plants and to express their creativity. It was also around this time that new garden designers, such as Garrett Eckbo and Roberto Burle Marx, were introducing ideas for outdoor spaces that had been explored in architecture a few decades earlier. And it is their designs that people still think of as modern, yet many were conceived 50 years ago.

People suddenly had their own yards, and the freedom to explore the world of plants

Contemporary color *(right)* Ted Smyth's design for architect Ron Sang's garden in Auckland, New Zealand, features curved walls in brilliant purple and pink, and a turquoise pool.

Pure pink *(below)* Luis Barragán found inspiration for the bright colors in his gardens in the Mexican countryside. These are reflected in the house he designed for Francisco Gilardi in Tacubaya, Mexico City.

Formal style

Originally a European tradition, formal gardens are about creating order and controlling nature. Symmetry and straight lines govern the style, while planting is often in the form of topiary or contained within geometric-shaped borders. One of the best examples is the vast parterre at Versailles, just outside Paris, France. Designed by André Le Nôtre for Louis XIV at the end of the 17th century, it represented the king's dominance over the landscape. The gardens at Hampton Court Palace in Surrey, England, are another fine example of formal style.

It is not surprising that formal gardens are associated with status and wealth, since the most famous are attached to palaces or stately homes. But their simplicity and the evergreen planting frequently used in formal designs provides year-

Perfectly formal (*bottom*) *The classic formal gardens at Villa Gamberaia in Tuscany, Italy, are among the best in the world.*

Beautiful box (*below*) *Kathy Brown's garden salutes French boxwood parterres and fountains.*

Terraces and topiary (*opposite*) *Originally designed by Penelope Hobhouse, this garden in London includes a formal lawn and borders on the upper terrace, and neat square beds and elegant pots on the lower level.*

round interest and can easily be scaled down to
fit small urban yards. Formal styles can also be
low-maintenance and suit today's lifestyles, in
which time is at a premium.

Some formal styles are associated with
particular religions. Traditional Islamic gardens
were divided by rills into four squares, each
contained within a small courtyard. The Alhambra
in Granada, Spain, is a good example. Islamic
gardens are still popular today, and elements of the
design translate well into contemporary spaces.

Current practitioners Renowned contemporary
designers who favor formality include Arabella
Lennox Boyd, Helen Dillon, and Sir Roy Strong.
Successful formal gardens today make use of
strong focal points and increasingly feature more
contemporary plants, such bamboo and tree ferns
in pots. Interior designer Kelly Hoppen has also
inspired a vogue for mixing in Asian influences.

Dynamic formality *(opposite, top) I used pencil-thin Italian cypresses as vertical accents and to contrast with rounder, softer-looking perimeter planting in this simple formal design.*

Jacobean elegance *(opposite, below) The gardens at Hatfield House, Hertfordshire, England, were originally designed by John Tradescant the Elder in the early 17th century.*

Loose formality *(above) These gardens attached to the 16th-century Herterton House in northeast England were designed in the late 1970s, and include formal topiary interspersed with loose drifts of flowers.*

Domed borders *(right) The pool at Wollerton Old Hall, Shropshire, England, is flanked by domes of box-wood and* Carpinus betulus *'Fastigiata'.*

Romantic style

For many people around the world, the romantic or cottage style is archetypally English. Whether it is represented by the sweeping grounds of a grand house or the tiny yard of a simple cottage, images of such gardens can be found on the lids of chocolate boxes and jigsaw puzzles almost everywhere, from North America to Australia.

Romantic, cottage gardens typically feature informal, curved beds, and lawns that act as soft, verdant carpets. Gently meandering pathways cut through swaths of planting, with the emphasis on flowering herbaceous plants, although fruit and vegetables are often included in the mix.

These gardens also make use of, or borrow, the landscapes beyond their boundaries. Focal points, such as church steeples, for example, are

Gentle, meandering paths cut through swaths of planting, with the emphasis on flowering herbaceous plants

Cottage chaos (this page)

Cottage gardens may look chaotic, but to achieve this look, plantings have to be carefully planned to keep the show going throughout summer. Rustic features, such as wooden fences and old pots, add to the effect.

Turrets and spires

(opposite page) The garden of Queen Elizabeth's former couturier, Sir Hardy Amies, is wildly romantic. The tiled turret of an out-building is hung with roses, and spires of hollyhocks punctuate the planting.

WHAT'S YOUR STYLE? **ROMANTIC**

incorporated into designs by the careful placing of plantings. Pavilions, gazebos, and furniture made from natural materials that complement the plantings play a part, too.

The hard landscaping is also natural, relying on wood, stone, gravel, and cobbles, usually put together with a handcrafted look.

Colorful places filled with flowers, romantic and cottage gardens are a plantsman's paradise. Gertrude Jekyll, William Robinson, Margery Fish, and Beatrix Potter are among the most famous practitioners, but their influence has spread farther afield to all forms of design— Laura Ashley's floral prints are a case in point.

Going global This relaxed style may be easy on the eye, but it is surprisingly difficult to achieve, requiring an in-depth knowledge of plant culture and visual effect. Like the words and actors in a play, the garden has to be carefully scripted and choreographed so that the particular talent of each of the players shines through.

The romantic style seems to go in and out of fashion every few years, and it is currently

Flowers and fowl (this page and opposite top) The romantic style uses loose, informal drifts of planting, with simple white daisies a popular choice for pots and borders. Wild flowers are occasionally mixed with cultivated varieties. Informal lawns, ponds, and roses or wisteria climbing up house walls also typify the style.

On the moor's edge (opposite, below) The garden of Sleightholmedale Lodge stands on the edge of England's Yorkshire moors, and has been cultivated and tended by the same family for three generations. The borders are overflowing with cottage garden favorites, such as poppies, foxgloves, campanulas, and lilies.

undergoing a renaissance. With its emphasis on nature and traditional home crafts, it represents an escape from technology and the manic pace of contemporary life.

Essentially a British style of design, the cottage garden has been exported across the globe, from North America to Japan, where borders overflowing with flowers are pursued with zeal.

With an emphasis on nature and home crafts, the style represents an escape from technology and the manic pace of life

Tropical style

Simple to define, a tropical-style garden is filled with large-leaved and colorful plants that make you feel as though you've just arrived in the tropics. Also known as "exotic" or "jungle," the popularity of this style is the result of more and more people traveling to far-flung locations, being inspired by what they see, and wanting to recreate their experiences at home.

Creating the effect Well suited to small or courtyard gardens, especially in cities, the tropical style is informal and relaxed, and often set off by brightly colored house walls or boundary fences.

Foliage plants dominate the plantings in these gardens. Those with deep, rich green and luxurious purple, red, and orange leaves achieve the right look, but remember that many exotics are not hardy and will need protection over winter in cold areas. That said, there are a number of subtropical plants that will withstand a light frost, including *Fatsia japonica, Cordyline australis*, and some palms, tree ferns, bamboos, and cannas. You could also try planting tender species in pots, which can be moved in winter, and positioning them around features, such as statues or small ponds. Look for nurseries that specialize in tropical plants and can offer good advice on their care.

Raymond Jungles, who creates gardens mainly in Florida, and Will Giles, a British designer, are among the best-known practitioners of this style.

Through the mist (*above right*) *Patrick Mahoney uses mist-making machines in his garden in Anaheim, California, both to increase humidity for the plants and to create a dramatic effect.*

The Essex tropics (*right*) *In his ambitious English garden, Paul Spracklin grows many exotics and xerophytes. The lookout, built on stilts, offers an elevated view of the garden.*

Balinese brilliance (right) Villa Bebek in Bali belongs to garden designer Made Wijaya. The complex includes a home, an office, and this garden adorned with lush plantings and tropical pools.

Jungle garden (below) Raymond Jungles' garden in Key West, Florida, is heavily influenced by the late renowned landscape architect Roberto Burle Marx, for whom he worked. Like Burle Marx, Jungles uses strong color to enhance his planting. His garden also includes murals designed and signed by his famous employer.

Wildlife gardens

More of a conviction than a style, looks aren't the first priority in a wildlife garden. Although there is usually some sense of order, neatness isn't the goal. As we become increasingly aware of the damage being done to the environment, in our own small way we can help redress the balance by giving nature a helping hand and creating welcoming habitats for wildlife in our gardens.

An eco-friendly gardener may install a pond to encourage frogs, toads, or salamanders, or use nectar-rich plants, such as buddleja and sedum, to attract bees and butterflies. But whatever plants you choose, leave them to complete their life cycle, from bud to decay, to support wildlife in all its forms. And avoid pesticides that damage the environment and kill beneficial insects, such as ladybugs and hoverflies, that prey on insect pests and guard your plants against attack.

Natural limits (bottom)
This mix of formal and wildlife styles shows great ingenuity. The naturalized grasses attract beneficial insects and birds that will keep pests away from the more formal planting.

Flower meadow (below)
Fired with red and yellow wild poppies and swaying grasses, this wonderful naturalistic garden in New Zealand paints a peaceful scene, and evokes a sense of harmony and well-being.

Wildlife gardens are not just for sandal-wearing hippies—they offer real benefits, reducing the need for harmful pesticides

Water world *(left)* Even a small pool will attract a whole range of animals and insects. Make sure at least one side of the pond has a sloping, beachlike edge. This allows small mammals and amphibians to scramble out if they fall in, and birds to bathe. Use oxygenating plants to keep the water clear.

Family affair *(above left and right)* Wildlife gardens are perfect for families (do not include ponds if you have young children). A paradise for butterflies, bees, and frogs, they awaken children's interest in the natural world, teaching them first-hand about the behavior and habitats of these creatures.

Asian style

The origins of this style can be traced back to ancient Chinese religious practices. Both Chinese religion and garden styles then traveled to Japan and were integrated into the national culture. The Asian garden as we know it today evolved from miniature landscapes, similar to bonsai, that were kept on the tables of China's elite. These tiny mountainscapes, complete with rivers and trees, were designed to provide a source of inspiration and emotional refreshment.

Mastering the art Deeply symbolic in the East, Asian gardens often lose their meaning when recreated in the West, where they may simply become beautiful pastiches. To avoid this, seek out books or visit gardens that help you to understand the symbolism of each of the garden's components and how they should be used.

Natural materials, such as wood, stone, and pebbles, are used for hard landscaping. Water—sometimes represented by gravel raked into meandering "streams"—also plays a part.

Key ingredients are flowering structural shrubs, including azaleas, and trees, such as cherries and Japanese maples, chosen for their delicate blossoms or for stunning fall color. Other plants, including hostas, mosses, bamboos, ferns, and grasses, are used for their foliage effects.

The importance of visual harmony in Asian gardens makes them ideal for small yards where the elements can be contained and balanced, but it can also be lovely to stumble across a secret Eastern corner within a larger garden.

Plants such as hostas, mosses, bamboos, and ferns are used for their foliage effects

Dappled light *(opposite top)* *Leaves and branches cast soft shadows and dappled sunlight on the grasses, topiary, and stone pathway of this Asian garden.*

Eastern show *(opposite bottom)* *Hiroshi Nanmori created this serene Japanese design for the 1996 RHS Chelsea Flower Show.*

Autumn flames *(above)* *At the Jojakko-ji temple in Kyoto, Japan, exquisite fall foliage colors set the garden ablaze.*

Far and wide *(left)* *The influence of Japanese garden design has spread to the four corners of the earth. This beautiful Asian-style garden by Ted Smyth is in Auckland, New Zealand.*

41

Self-sufficient style

A method rather than style of gardening, self-sufficiency is all about growing your own food. It is a reaction to modern life and an alternative to factory farming, appealing to those who are concerned about what they eat, where and how their food is produced, and, as part of the bigger picture, the way the environment is being degraded. Although many supermarkets offer a choice of fresh, free-range, and organic food, which is available year-round, it comes at a high price. But for relatively little outlay, self-sufficiency is a more attractive, less expensive option, if you have the interest and time to spare.

Food ethics The increasing popularity of local farmers' markets—both in cities and in small towns—points to the fact that people not only appreciate tastier food, but are also asking questions about production methods, including the use of any chemicals and how livestock is kept. Growing your own fruit and vegetables is just taking this idea of choice one step further. It's about using your yard, however large or small, to put food on your table.

One of my favorite TV comedies from the 1970s was *The Good Life*, in which the central characters, Tom and Barbara Good, give up their jobs for a life of suburban self-sufficiency. The idea is alluring, and although it may be too radical for most of us, growing some of your own food is hugely rewarding—and great fun.

Growing your own food is a reaction to modern life and an alternative to factory farming

Going organic (*above*)
This productive organic vegetable patch in north London shows that even a small yard in the city offers space for some home-grown fruit and vegetables.

Potager paradise (*right*)
Stalks of white and red Swiss chard dominate this colorful potager, where fat pumpkins decorate tall obelisks and pretty flowers attract pollinating insects.

Roof gardens *(left)* These ingenious grass-roofed buildings in Norway offer cheap insulation in the harsh winter months, and food for birds and insects in the summer.

Fall harvest *(below)* This garden at Rofford Manor, Worcestershire, England, shows that self-sufficiency can be beautiful as well as productive. In early fall, the walled garden is a riot of color, and bursting with crops ready for harvesting.

New World style

This means a number of different things, but mainly it's about looking to warmer continents where people, freed from the constraints of temperamental weather conditions, enjoy an outdoor way of life. With its glorious climate, Australia is a prime example. Very much at the forefront of the New World style, it is an unashamedly modern country that's uninhibited by European architectural and garden design traditions. Australians have a close and relaxed relationship with their gardens, regarding their "outdoor room" as an extension of their home.

Heading West North America is full of inspiration, too, whether it is wooden water towers on top of skyscrapers, Colorado mountains, quirky Venice Beach, or the Florida Everglades.

I am also influenced by those photographs of 1950s Hollywood stars posing in the beautifully manicured gardens of their mansions in Beverly Hills. These aspirational images encapsulate the glamour and glitz of the American dream, and are fun to recreate in modern gardens.

Two other influential planting styles have recently emerged from North America. The first takes its inspiration from the wide-open prairies of pioneer days. The designs mimic the mix of wild flowers and waving grasses, and also bring to mind huge fields of crops in the Midwest. At the other end of the style scale are the glamorous formal roof gardens of Manhattan and Seattle.

Weather conditions across the continents vary hugely, but whatever the climate, the essence of the New World style is the sense of freedom and freshness that pervades these designs.

Beach life (left) Salt-laden, windswept grasses and scattered rocks mirror the naturalized plants on the beach beyond this garden. Designed by Ted Smyth, the low, subtle planting in this garden in New Zealand allows an uninterrupted view of the roaring ocean.

Flying high (above) The roof of this structure in Steve Martino's design for the Stiteler Garden in Tucson, Arizona, is reminiscent of the wings of an airplane. This effect is intensified by the bird's-eye views from the elevated deck of the vast landscape below.

View from the deck (left)
This simple deck offers a platform from which to admire the landscape below. The design is very simple and doesn't compete with the spectacular views.

Poolside paradise (below)
Designed by Raymond Jungles, this poolside garden in Montifiore, Florida, follows the rectilinear shape of the pool itself, from the simple bench strewn with colorful cushions, to the neatly trimmed lawn and the low-growing hedge that frames the water.

Surreal style

For me, the word "surreal" can describe many quirky and odd things, and is epitomized by the paintings, and indeed the life, of Salvador Dalí. Many art forms have had surreal periods, and thankfully garden design is no exception. Surreal ideas include the folk art of Irish farmers' wives, who painted small, round stones white and placed them on walls as decoration, and the Victorian obsession with miniature versions of mountains, such as the Matterhorn, that fed the public's appetite for exploration and discovery. Even the ongoing fascination with garden gnomes can be classified as surreal. All these weird garden designs set their creators apart from the crowd.

Breaking the rules There are no set rules about what makes a garden surreal: the design could rely on a mass of unusual plants grouped together, or structures that are dramatically over- or undersized. But most surreal gardens have to be seen first-hand to be explained.

My favorite surrealist designers are Charles Jencks, Ivan Hicks, and Tony Heywood, but I also love the work of others who dare to be different. There's the garden filled with hundreds of gnomes, and one lady in London whose yard is an homage to Barbie dolls, for example.

My advice is to enjoy creating your garden, and if that results in something weird or surreal, great—but don't force it.

Lollipop land (above) Parts of the Hanging Gardens at Marqueyssac in the Dordogne, France, are fabulously wacky. Classified as a historical monument, they include rockeries and waterfalls, and more than three-and-a-half miles (six kilometers) of pathways, edged with 150,000 hand-trimmed boxwood plants clipped into strange designs.

Monster topiary (right) This crazy topiary creature— which reminds me of the Loch Ness monster—seems to dip into and rise out of this New Zealand garden. Topiary is versatile and doesn't always have to be clipped into formal shapes. With a little imagination, it can be used to carve out giant birds or imaginary creatures like this one.

Bursts of color *(far left) Tony Heywood is one of my favorite surrealist gardeners. This colorful and wacky conceptual garden is a testament to his wild imagination.*

Trick of the eye *(left) This trompe l'oeil doorway appears to offer a view through to a flower-studded garden.*

Thigh high *(below) Ivan Hicks creates humorous and free-spirited gardens that catch your eye and make you think twice about what you're looking at. I find his work, such as this canoe filled with models of human legs, inspirational.*

Spiritual style

Deeply personal and now mostly secular, spiritual style originated as an expression of religious feeling. Iconic medieval, Islamic, and Japanese Zen gardens are hugely influential, having provided some of the main inspirations for garden styles in general, and in particular the notion of an outdoor space as a place for quiet contemplation.

Creating harmony A respect for life in all its forms is at the heart of the spiritual garden, and this is most likely to be reflected in the plantings, which are usually simple and restrained.

Such gardens also feature objects that are used as focal points for meditation. These include statues (representations of Buddha are popular), grottoes complete with images of the Virgin Mary, or water features. Most spiritual gardens are enclosed and secluded, with seating for the gardener and visitor alike.

There are also New Age gardens—such as the one at Chalice Well in Somerset, England, where trees are particularly significant—and healing gardens, which are often designed as peaceful sanctuaries for hospitals and hospices.

Serene and simple
(opposite top) Luciano Giubbilei's geometric garden designs evoke serenity.

Landscape in miniature
(opposite bottom) Joanna Mowbray and Bruno Roméda's design includes symbolic rills and sculpture.

Get close to nature *(left) There's nothing like feeling earth in your hands, but if you don't want to get grubby, try hugging a tree.*

Monumental *(above)*
The gardens of the Musée Albert-Kahn in Boulogne-Billancourt, France, were first built in 1895, partly by Achille Duchêne, but new projects continue to this day. This Pyramid of Pebbles by Takano Fumiako looks like an ancient monument rising up from the earth. Trees, shrubs, mosses, and lichens are used to integrate the pyramid into the landscape.

Family style

The idea of the nuclear family with two kids and a dog is a little out of date. Many people are juggling the demands of their own children and stepchildren of widely differing ages. This places pressure on you as the garden designer to meet all their needs. As outlined in Chapter 1, start by listing everyone's likes and dislikes, and then note down the whole family's needs.

All-around winner The list of "must-haves" for most families is a long one. Requirements may include paved areas where the kids can cycle or skateboard, swings and slides, places to sunbathe and enjoy a drink, party areas, the barbecue grill, or space for teenagers to entertain their friends. If you don't have a garage, you need places to stash your garbage cans, bicycles, lawnmowers and other gardening paraphernalia, and, when they're not in use, trampolines or wading pools. And all of this has to be worked together into a cohesive and stylish design.

One of the keys to a successful family garden is to create a space that both entertains and informs your children. Try to include interesting planting for adults to enjoy, alongside areas that the children can cultivate themselves. And give the young ones a few vegetables or fruits to plant and nurture—learning about how food is grown will broaden their experience of life.

Ultimately, it's a question of defining areas for different members of the family to enjoy, and coming up with a plan that is clear and concise.

The key to success is to create a garden that both entertains and informs your children

Swing low (left) Simon Fraser's design features a child's swing attached to an arbor, merging the adults' and children's space and avoiding the more common segregation of areas.

Getting together (below) Eating together as a family on a warm summer evening is a wonderful experience— it offers everyone a chance to catch up and chat, and is really relaxing, too.

Something for everyone (below left) This garden in London, designed by Jill Billington and Mimi Harris, has lots of space for the kids to run around and for adults to gather and relax.

Functional sculpture (opposite page) This fun structure is a jungle gym, slide, and swing all in one, but the materials used and the overall plan are so well thought out that the finished design seems almost sculptural. When buying play equipment, remember that young children soon grow out of small slides and swings, so it may be best to look for inexpensive items that can be easily replaced as they grow.

3
The big picture

Well-designed gardens all have a unifying principle, a central idea that creates a cohesive, integrated look. **To produce beautiful designs**, let's depart from the Victorian notion of including lots of different elements in the garden just because we can. It's tempting to rush out and buy plants, gnomes, birdbaths, and water features that have no relation to one another, and then dot them around the yard. But the results look messy and unfocused—they lack a big idea to bind the design together.

To avoid this mistake, **establish an overall look** for your garden at the planning stage, and get a feeling for the essence of your design. The essence is conveyed when visitors take a glance at the garden and immediately understand what it's all about. It should also reveal something about your personal style.

Take, for example, a garden with a central, rectangular lawn, flanked by neat shrub borders, with **a large urn on a pedestal** at the end. You instantly know this is a formal space, governed by clean lines, and designed by someone with a clear vision who likes order. An informal garden with a winding path flowing through borders of grasses and wild flowers produces a very different image, yet it still has **a cohesive design**—the big picture is clearly drawn and understood.

But the big picture doesn't have to be a specific style, such as romantic, contemporary, or Japanese. You may be influenced by these ideas, and then adapt them to suit you. The most important thing to keep in mind is that your design should be coherent: it should lead visitors around your space, **show them where to look**, and, most of all, reflect your personality and individual style. To help you to understand this concept, let's analyze a selection of well-designed gardens and figure out the idea behind the big picture.

Establish an overall look for your garden at the planning stage, and get a feeling for the essence of your design

Vibrant family garden

Show gardens are, by definition, big statement exhibits, usually with a central theme. The overall concept for my design for the 2004 RHS Chelsea Flower Show is a family garden; my objective is to create a vibrant plan that's fun, immediate, and has a certain levity.

Diverse inspirations Designed as a suburban Eden, I have taken inspiration from themes as diverse as the Festival of Britain, Roald Dahl's *Charlie and the Chocolate Factory*, and Tasmanian landscapes. With a wave of brightly colored metal lollipops weaving through it, the garden is an experiment in color. The lollipops are both sculptural and useful as garden dividers; they also help to direct visitors around the space.

The oval pavilion looks like a jeweled Fabergé egg, and is covered with 5,000 enameled metal spheres, which echo those on the pergola. Spheres and spots—popular in contemporary art and design, from Damien Hurst's paintings to fashion, textile, and graphic design—link all the elements in the garden to create the big picture.

A sinuous pathway, composed of floating paved circles, links together all the features in the garden

The big picture

This garden is an example of a design with a cohesive idea. The spheres and circles, which link the features, the hard landscaping, and the architecture, unify the design. You immediately understand that this is no formal space, but a garden for playing and parties, and generally having fun outside.

The colored spheres cast circular shadows onto the circular paving, repeating the imagery used in the garden

The pavilion is a piece of functional sculpture, and could be used as a summerhouse, an office, or a playroom

Linked circular paving, reminiscent of flying saucers, snakes to the pavilion at the back of the garden

The pavilion door lowers to form an oval patio that connects with the pathway

Ferns and grasses soften the hard landscaping and bind the features together

City oasis

Restful and feminine, this is not an ostentatious garden, but shows the owner's passion for growing and displaying a wide variety of plants. The planting has a hint of the exotic, but it could easily be changed to follow a different style, without the need to alter the overall structure.

Interlinking circles This is a good, strong design. The visitor understands that this garden is all about enjoying the plants in a secluded, restful environment. Circles link the elements here: a

round lawn leads down to a paved area featuring a circular, raised pond. The same color and type of paving has been used throughout to create a feeling of coherence and cohesion.

A narrow pathway cuts through the beds at the back of the garden, invoking an element of intrigue, while dense planting all around the perimeter adds a sense of secrecy and security. Additional interest is provided by the figurative sculptures and dramatic foliage shapes and colors. This is a practical design that's easy to negotiate and very beautiful.

The big picture

Owned and designed by artist Camilla Shivarg, this garden is used to display her sculptures. Situated in west London, it is a secret oasis, screened from the neighbors and traffic noise. The well-balanced planting plan, integrated hard landscaping, and unifying shapes create a coherent, comfortable garden.

The round lawn at the center of the design visually pulls the other elements together

An informal path forms a harmonious transition from the hard paving of the patio to the soft grass

The steps up to the lawn provide a strong sense of direction, while their chevron shape makes a small statement

Colorful plantings, including penstemons, cannas, and phormiums, create a beautiful exotic display in the borders

A circular pond, half hidden beneath a mass of foliage, mirrors the sky and echoes the lawn

Topiary garden

The planting in this garden is surreal, which is why I love it. The design displays a wonderful eccentricity because it marries two completely different styles, yet they fit together perfectly.

A beautiful old apple tree, which has obviously occupied this space for many years, forms the main focal point, and is underplanted with a drift of Robinsonian naturalistic, woodland planting.

In sharp contrast, the almost military lineup of clipped boxwood spheres look as though they are on parade, standing to attention on the lawn in front of the elegant historic house.

Year-round interest The juxtaposition of planting styles entertains and startles, and the tree and spheres create a design that's sustainable all year—when the herbaceous planting dies down in winter, the fantastic structure of the balls comes into play. This is a contemporary design that has been integrated into a garden that has evolved slowly over time.

The big picture

Created by garden designer and writer Fiona Lawrenson, this private garden in Sussex is contemporary in its true sense. Contemporary style doesn't have to mean steel and glass; it can, as shown here, mean a new interpretation of a traditional topiary and flower garden. This is the big idea.

Elegant square pots,
featuring cone-shaped
topiary, frame the door
and bring the planting
right up to the house

A wooden obelisk
mirrors the conical
topiary, and adds a
vertical element to
this part of the design

Boxwood spheres
are laid out in a strictly
formal pattern, and
cast intriguing shadows
across the smooth lawn

The subtle purples,
lilacs, and pinks in this
border contrast with
the sharp outlines of
the dark green spheres

An old apple tree
heightens the humor in
the garden—when ripe
apples fall, they mimic
the boxwood balls

Multilevel garden

The big idea here is a restful, secluded space, unified with decorative foliage and very few hard landscaping materials. Essentially low-maintenance, the plants have been designed for maximum interest—tall trees line the boundaries, screening neighbors on either side, while shorter clipped shrubs create more intimate areas within the garden. The design also has a dynamic quality, with steep wooden steps and terraces that lead you through the space.

Hidden depths Set on a hillside, this plan makes the most of an awkward, sloping site. What we see here is only part of a larger space; the garden continues down the steps in the foreground to a secluded area behind the deck, creating two fantastic plant-based garden rooms. Visible from the upper terraces, a beautiful eucalyptus tree offers a dramatic focal point at the end of the yard, while its evergreen foliage helps to screen the tall buildings behind.

The terrace features an elegant table and chairs in a contrasting style to the rest of the setting. The area is screened by a retaining wall, and offers the perfect spot to enjoy a glass of wine.

The big picture

A cleverly planned solution for an awkward yard, this garden in San Francisco was designed by Chris Jacobsen. Overlooked by tall buildings, the planting maintains a sense of seclusion and intrigue. Wooden steps and decks unite the space, and take you on an interesting journey through the garden.

Tall trees and shrubs have been used along the boundaries to create living walls that offer interest and total privacy

The decked terrace is screened by a neatly clipped pittosporum hedge, which has colorful foliage

The decorative furniture emulates an ornate Regency style which, although at odds with the garden as a whole, works well as a contrast

Wooden paths and steps have a warmth and texture that complements the foliage plants that spill on to them

Plantswoman's garden

When I first visited Helen Dillon's garden, there was a carpet of lawn between the hot- and cool-colored borders. She has replaced this with sleek paving and a canal of reflecting water—a master stroke that has changed the whole feel of the design. This is a garden for plant lovers, and cleverly combines traditional and modern styles. The conservatory, clipped hedges, and borders follow old-fashioned lines, while the clean, sleek shape of the canal speaks of something more recent. A wide garden, the space is framed with planting to create a more intimate mood.

The big picture

Helen Dillon's Dublin garden is open to visitors, and performs well as both a private and a public space. Its very simple design combines the current trend for minimalism with more traditional elements to create a cohesive, elegant picture. A really good update of a classic style, the deep borders are luxuriously indulgent, and the large pool creates a sense of serenity.

The canal leads the eye down the center of the garden to an arbor hung with flowers

The formality and symmetrical layout of the garden are softened by herbaceous borders

A blue border that flanks the water forms a cool contrast to the fiery beds opposite

Vertical accents of yew create dramatic focal points within the herbaceous borders

Topiary cones punctuate the end of the hot, fiery border

Pale stone paving forms a neutral foil to the intense colors and textures in the borders

Modern elevated garden

This contemporary garden reflects new directions, in both the planting plans and the materials used. The space is obviously designed for entertaining and relaxing outside, and this represents the essence of a new garden movement.

Focal point Rather than drawing your eye to the back of the yard, the design focuses it across the space on a diagonal. The pavilion in the far corner provides a focal point, its geometric shape accentuated by the garden's subtle layers, formed by elevated flowerbeds that seem to hover above the ground like floating steel-edged trays.

Still relatively new, the planting hasn't yet had time to mature and fulfill its potential of creating green screens. The use of traditional walling and paving stones conflicts with the more modern elements, and better results may have been achieved by rendering and painting the walls. However, the garden still represents an interesting and exciting modern space.

The big picture

The horizontal lines of the steps and raised beds are reinforced by a modern slatted trellis on the back wall, which helps to soften the hard landscaping and holds the design together. Very simple and very urban, this garden will, in time, become an oasis of green with slight hints of contemporary structure.

The large-leaved climber, *Vitis coignetiae*, or crimson glory vine, has spectacular fall color, and will eventually cover the trellis

The table and benches mirror the design of the box-like raised beds and terraces, offering a harmonious marriage of form and function

Wide, shallow steps climb gently to the top of the yard, adding to the linear effect created by the terraces

Mass plantings of lavender, with its blue-gray evergreen foliage, create a broad sweep of color and structure in this bed

The terraces look like trays floating one above the other, while the soft blue-gray color helps to soften the strong lines

Contemporary roof terrace

Reminiscent of a colonial garden, or a terrace in the Bahamas, this design is actually on a roof in Soho in the heart of London. A contemporary outdoor living room, the garden is a relaxing space, screened from the noise and bustle of the streets below by lush, subtropical planting.

Planned on a simple cross, the symmetrical design is restful, and infuses the space with a calming atmosphere. Decking provides a soft, warm floor, and in each corner, skylights, which allow light into the rooms below during the day, illuminate the garden at night.

The planting is influenced by the tropics, and includes large bananas, bamboo, and palms that thrive in this sheltered city microclimate. The plants and features hint at opulence and wealth.

The big picture

Designed by John Bailey, this garden evokes a colonial era, when time passed slowly and hot days were spent sipping drinks on a shady terrace. In direct contrast with the noisy city streets below, this tranquil, exotic oasis combines a nostalgic ambience with contemporary design influences.

Bold, subtropical plants create an exotic flavor, and heighten the drama with their architectural foliage

Subtle elevations split the garden into separate areas and increase the illusion of space

A central dining area gives the garden a useful focal point, both visually and practically

The large skylights were a potential problem but have been cleverly integrated into the new garden design

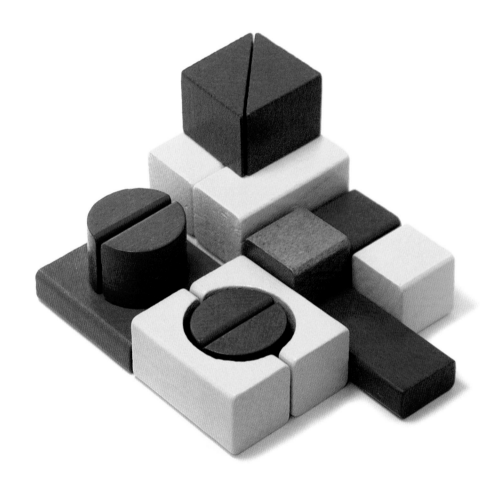

4

Line and shape

Some of the best garden designs are based on strong lines and shapes, which determine the style, proportions, and movement in the garden. The line of a garden usually refers to a path or route that leads the eye and **directs you through the space**, but in some cases, it forms the basis of the ground plan, and may be less obvious in the final design.

Lines impose order and offer clarity, helping to control the overall look of the garden, while shapes and volumes fill the spaces between them. Rather like laying a rug in the middle of a floor, shapes also provide **definition and pattern**, and create space for you to stand at a distance and appreciate the different features of your garden.

Shapes and lines signify the style of your design, too. Curved lines and oval shapes usually give a garden an informal appearance, while straight lines, squares, and rectangles generally confer formality. Lines and shapes can also divide up a yard into smaller spaces, with **proportions that feel more comfortable** for the human body.

To design your lines, start by sketching a rough outline of your garden on a letter-size piece of paper, and photocopy it a few times. Then look through this chapter for ideas on the best lines to use, and start experimenting. The main pitfall is to base your designs on complicated and fussy shapes, which are difficult to navigate. Practice drawing broad, sweeping curves or **strong straight lines** that make the most of the space, and try to get the proportions right. Think about directing the eye away from the boundaries, unless you have a good view—in which case, create lines that flow toward the vista. And consider how your lines will come to a stop—they should always **end with a focal point**, be that a specimen tree, beautiful flower border, or piece of sculpture. When you are happy with your lines, fit in shapes around them that are sympathetic to the mood you have created.

Lines impose order and offer clarity, helping to control the overall look of the garden, while shapes and volumes fill the spaces between them

Using lines

When garden designers talk about "line," they generally mean the path or route through the garden, although the term also refers to the line traced by other features and plantings.

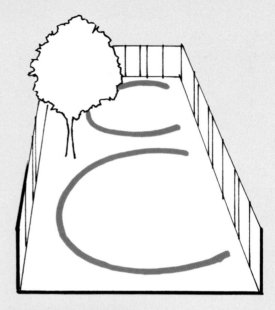

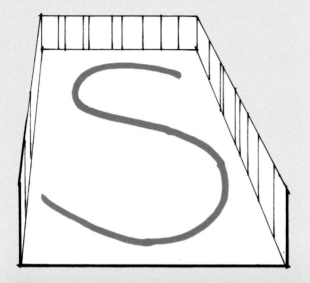

S- and C-curves

These lines are fluid and offer great scope for informal and naturalistic designs. They take the eye from one side of the garden to the other, amplifying the space and making small gardens appear larger. Flowing lines also create a sense of momentum and movement.

Snakes and curves *This small town garden (above) shows how a flowing S-curve can extend the route through a yard, and trick the eye into thinking the space is larger than it is. Here, a circular pool slots perfectly into the first curve, forming a pleasing coupling of line and shape, while the tight turn of the second bend quickens the pace. The informal suburban garden (right) is based on two C-shapes with circular lawns cupped within them.*

Crosses

Straight lines set in a cross were traditionally used in Islamic gardens, French parterres, and formal styles of the 17th and 18th centuries. Crosses lead the eye to the end of the garden and are suitable for large yards. Contemporary designers often shift the central line to create asymmetry.

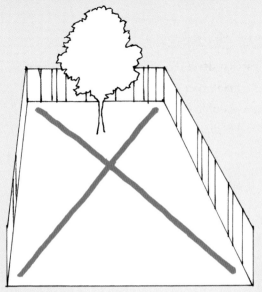

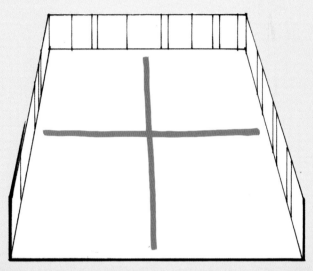

Diagonals

Diagonal lines have more energy and movement than crosses. They can evoke formality but may also form the basis of informal, asymmetrical designs. They work well in small yards because they take the eye across the garden at its longest point; diagonal lines are often employed in contemporary urban designs where space is limited.

Straight to the point *Laid out on a cross, this recent take on a French parterre (above) has been designed with wonderful symmetry and great clarity of vision. The smaller garden (right) shows how even a tiny yard can emulate the grand styles of large formal designs. By setting the paths and planting along diagonal lines, the garden maximizes the available space.*

Using shapes

Unlike lines, which cut or weave through your space, shapes create blocks of soft or hard landscaping. Choose symmetrical geometric shapes for formal designs, or organic, fluid forms for informal or naturalistic garden styles.

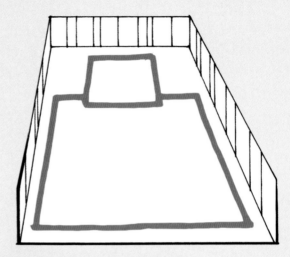

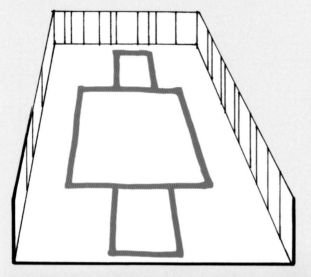

Rectangles and squares

These shapes provide an excellent framework for almost any garden, large or small. Use them in the center of your space to create a formal design, or lay a series of them on a diagonal across the yard to create a more relaxed look. You could also link squares and rectangles in a large yard, or combine them with a circle, and allow planting to spill over the sides to soften their sharp edges.

Layering rectangles and squares *Based on a cross, the different-sized rectangles used in this small garden (above) are linked to create a cohesive, attractive design. The focus is a central rectangular lawn, set off with a brick mowing edge. The Zen garden (right) is based on squares, which convey a neat formality. The pavers line up with the garden room and seat, and all the elements work together to form a harmonious whole.*

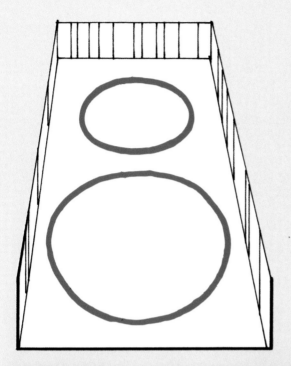

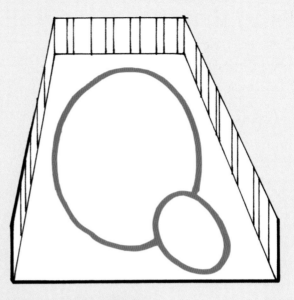

Circles and ellipses

Both of these shapes draw the eye into the center of the garden, visually widening spaces and making them seem more open. Ellipses give a more informal impression than squares and rectangles, although circles can be used both for formal and informal styles.

Formal circles and relaxed ellipse *A long, narrow urban garden (left) is broken up with a series of circles into more usable spaces. The shapes are laid along a central axis, creating a formal appearance. They also focus the eye toward the center of the space, making the yard look wider, and add a fluidity to the design, which squares and rectangles often lack. The elliptical deck in the small terrace (above) works in a similar way, pulling the eye away from the edges, though in this case, the materials and shape convey informality.*

77

Large gardens and square yards

If you're feeling a bit daunted by the thought of designing a large garden, don't be! The trick is to decide whether you want to retain a sense of openness, or close things up and create intrigue by designing a series of smaller garden rooms.

Draw a rough sketch of your garden (*see p113*), photocopy it lots of times, and then just draw very simple lines on it. Remember that flowing lines give an informal appearance, while rigid crosses are more formal. Think, too, about how your lines and shapes will move you around the garden. Sharp corners are uncomfortable;

gentle changes in direction are best. Use strong shapes to create a focus, and bold planting along the perimeters, to prevent your yard from resembling a field.

Pure and simple *The appeal of this garden is its simplicity. A rectangular lawn provides a foil for the exuberant planting to either side, and draws the focus toward the pond and archway.*

Exaggerating the space

The simple design flows around the house and leads the eye away from the boundaries with the help of strategically placed planting. The large oval lawn creates an open area that celebrates the feeling of space.

Laid on a diagonal, the oval lawn creates a long vista and a sense of openness and space

Sinuous curves control the space, leading the visitor first to the house and then on a leafy walk around to the backyard

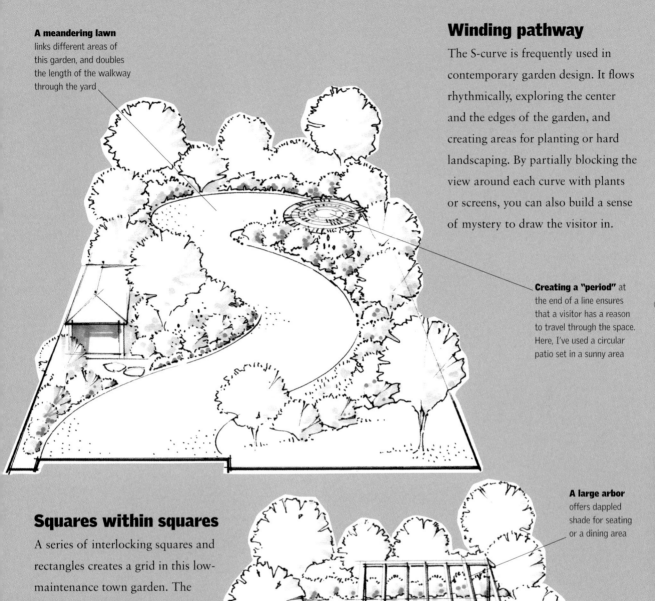

A meandering lawn
links different areas of
this garden, and doubles
the length of the walkway
through the yard

Winding pathway

The S-curve is frequently used in
contemporary garden design. It flows
rhythmically, exploring the center
and the edges of the garden, and
creating areas for planting or hard
landscaping. By partially blocking the
view around each curve with plants
or screens, you can also build a sense
of mystery to draw the visitor in.

Creating a "period" at
the end of a line ensures
that a visitor has a reason
to travel through the space.
Here, I've used a circular
patio set in a sunny area

A large arbor
offers dappled
shade for seating
or a dining area

Squares within squares

A series of interlocking squares and
rectangles creates a grid in this low-
maintenance town garden. The
perimeter is planted with shrubs
and trees, so the eye is focused
into the center. The arbor,
designed as a main feature,
shades this sunny site.

The angular shapes
of the beds, borders, and
paved area mirror the
square-shaped yard and
evoke a semi-formal look

Small spaces

You have to be clever with small gardens to create something simple and uncomplicated in the limited space available. A small yard is, in effect, a courtyard garden, and the four examples below, all of the same size and proportion, have been designed to illustrate just how many different effects can be achieved within such tight boundaries. A good rule of thumb is not to design anything too busy, and avoid too many decorative elements. Instead, stick to one main idea, and then follow it through by laying down simple lines and shapes. Focus on contrasting the textures of different materials, and always remember, less is more.

Miniature design *A diagonal line bisects this tiny courtyard to create a simple, but not soulless, patio garden.*

The garden room provides the main focus in this design

Simple squares

The surface materials used to create the squares here could be lawn or paving, or a combination. Your choice would depend on where you needed a hard surface for seating or a dining area.

The lawn is broken up into two distinct areas with paving slabs and low planting to create an elegant design

The perimeter planting in this formal yard combines sizable shrubs and trees to deflect attention away from the stark boundary fences

Following the curve

The C-curve swings past the garden room, which is the main focal point, to a statue or feature plant hidden from view at the end of the yard.

Garden of rectangles

This small garden shows the kind of minimal design that was popular in the '90s. Rectangles and squares, confined within low walls, convey a very angular look, although the harsh lines are softened by use of delicate pinks and mauves. The natural stone and pebble floor add to its elegance.

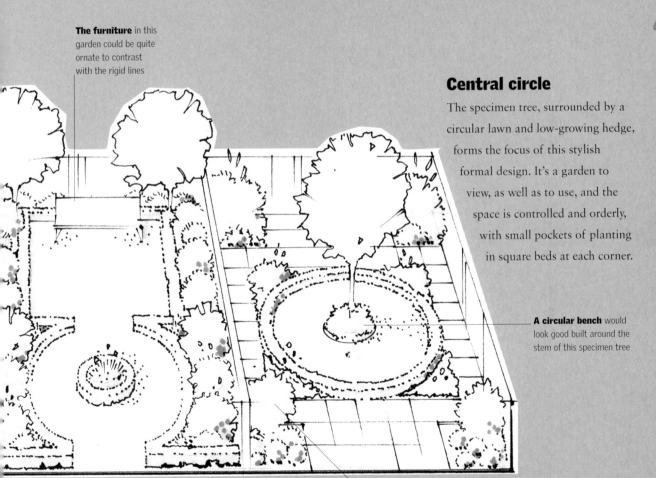

The furniture in this garden could be quite ornate to contrast with the rigid lines

Central circle

The specimen tree, surrounded by a circular lawn and low-growing hedge, forms the focus of this stylish formal design. It's a garden to view, as well as to use, and the space is controlled and orderly, with small pockets of planting in square beds at each corner.

A circular bench would look good built around the stem of this specimen tree

Mix and match

A square and circle form the basis of this Victorian-style garden. A pool and bench are focal points, and the beds are edged with clipped boxwood.

Topiary bay trees add to the feeling of formality and order, as does the low boxwood hedge edging the lawn

81

Long, thin yards

Town and city gardens tend to be thin rectangles because they are squeezed between neighboring yards. Without careful planning, they may end up looking like tunnels, but you can avoid this by using line and shape to direct the focus away from the boundaries and into the center. Rectangles laid on a diagonal or circles set on an S-curve are two ways of achieving this end.

Hints of formality *(right) This town garden, divided by low hedges, is technically flawed because the formal rectangles have scalloped edges, yet it still has charm.*

The summerhouse has two aspects: it looks out over lawn and beds in one direction, and the play area in the other

Rectangles on diagonal lines

One rectangle running down the center of a long, thin yard will make it look even longer and thinner, but when set on a diagonal, rectangles have the opposite effect and create a strong sense of direction. The design here offers three separate rooms, which could be laid with lawn or paving.

The triangular spaces along the boundary walls are perfect for beds or even, as in this instance, a pond

Garden of circles

Circles work particularly well in narrow gardens, since the eye is naturally drawn around the curves and away from the boundaries. This design uses circles set on an S-curve, offering the best of both line and shape. By masking some areas from view, it also heightens the mystery.

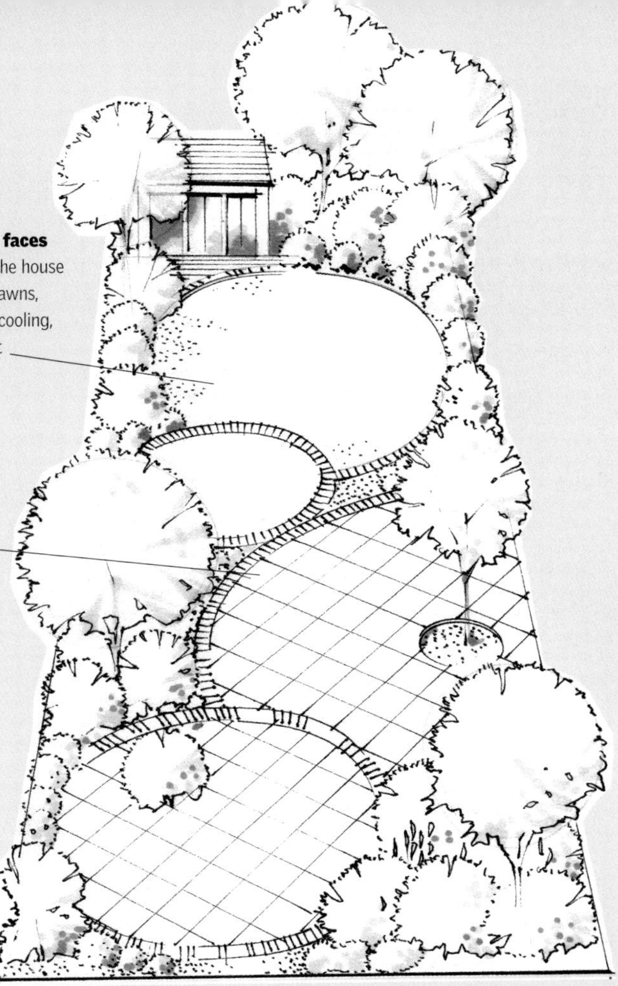

The pavilion faces back toward the house over circular lawns, which have a cooling, relaxing effect

Large paved areas, edged with planting, offer hard surfaces for a dining room and seating area, and help to reduce maintenance

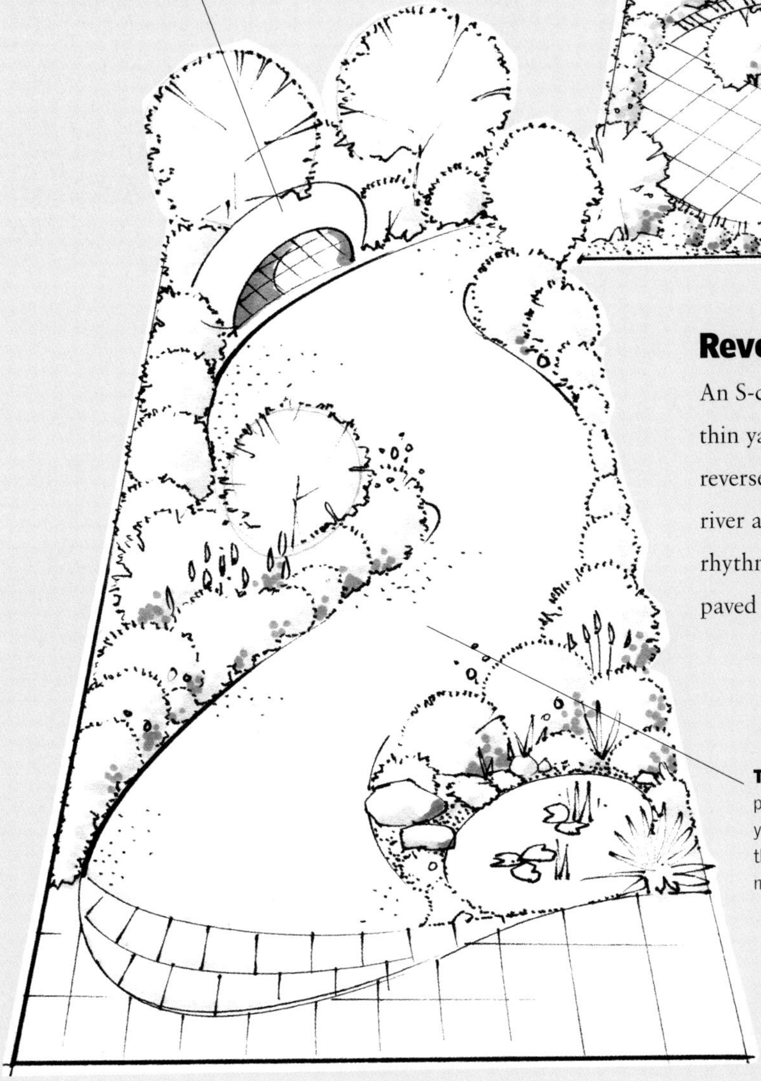

This pavilion or sun shelter is contemporary in style, and its curved, cavelike shape echoes the garden's flowing lines

Reversed S-shape

An S-curve is perfect for an informal long, thin yard, whether it is the right way around or reversed, as shown here. The line evokes a flowing river and the design resonates with a dynamic rhythm. Sweeping steps run down from a curved paved patio, unifying the line and shape.

The fluid lines of the lawn allow the planting to drift out into the center of the yard, breaking up the view and lengthening the perspective. A small circular pool tucks neatly in between the lawn and patio

Shallow, wide yards

Of all the garden shapes, wide, shallow yards can be the most demanding to design. The main stumbling block is that when viewing the garden from the house, you are looking across the shortest distance toward the back fence or your neighbor's yard. This means that even if you have a large space overall, it is difficult to appreciate the total size. To counter this problem, you have to control the line with great care.

Diagonal lines are the best solution. They lead the eye from one side of the yard across to the farthest corner, lengthening the perspective, while plants can be used to mask the boundaries. Or you could try to keep all the focus in the center of the yard.

Central focus *Squares of boxwood set in a symmetrical pattern create a quirky display that keeps the focus in the center of the yard. A simple idea, it's designed with a humorous touch.*

Elliptical center

Based on a diagonal line and smooth oval shape, this garden obeys fundamental design rules, skewing the perspective to deflect attention away from the back fence. The patio leads you to the far end of the ellipse, which is encircled by lush plantings, forcing you to look back toward the house.

Set on a diagonal and looking out across the garden, this sun room offers privacy and adds a beautiful focal point

Tall trees and shrubs shield the fence from view and keep the site from being overlooked

The curved deck leads out to the oval lawn and presents a vista across the grass to the garden room on the other side

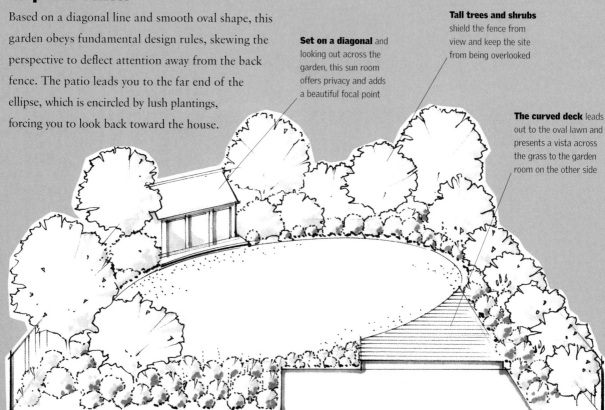

Elegant diamonds

Using squares layered on top of each other and set on their sides redefines the whole garden space and generates a new energy. The top square could be a paved terrace and the bottom a lawn area moving into gravel. The materials and right angles also help to direct the eye away from the perimeter.

Overlapping squares set on a diagonal open up the space and boost the energy of the design

Angled shapes create pockets for planting or a garden room or shed

Stretched "S"

Elongating an S-shape across the garden has the same effect as running it down the center, diverting the focus and making the most of the space. Here, the wide stepped terrace leads down to the lawn and across to a gazebo.

The broad sweeping "S" is punctuated by a gazebo, which offers a good vantage point from which to view the garden

The beds and borders hug the edge of the lawn, while large trees pull the eye to the corners of the yard

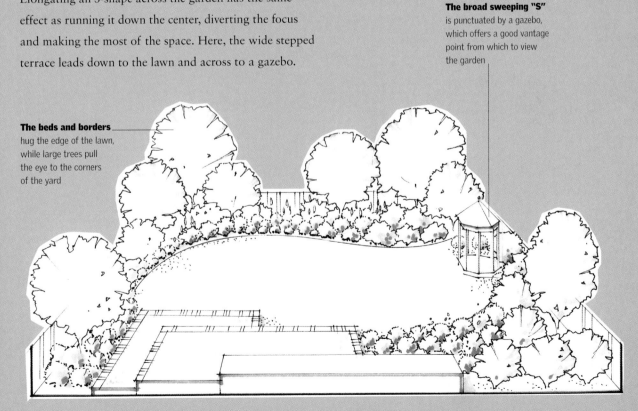

85

L-shaped gardens

Especially common in urban or city situations, L-shaped gardens are among the most awkward yards to deal with. They create two separate areas that have very little connection with each other, so the real trick is in unifying the parts. You can do this in several ways, using lines and shapes, plantings and hard landscaping materials, to create a harmonious space and lead people through the garden. The most difficult L-shape to design is where there is a narrow corridor running down the side of the house. It appears to be a walkway leading nowhere, and, in many cases, doesn't get much sun, making it dark and gloomy. In this instance, clever use of line and shape is essential to successfully integrate the corridor into the main part of the garden.

Clever use of space (right) *Good-quality materials and different levels create interest in this wonderful garden. A series of rectangles links a narrow section with the main garden, and strikes a balance between plants and decking.*

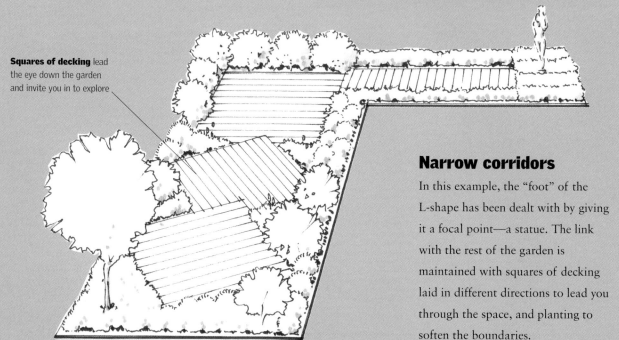

Squares of decking lead the eye down the garden and invite you in to explore

Narrow corridors

In this example, the "foot" of the L-shape has been dealt with by giving it a focal point—a statue. The link with the rest of the garden is maintained with squares of decking laid in different directions to lead you through the space, and planting to soften the boundaries.

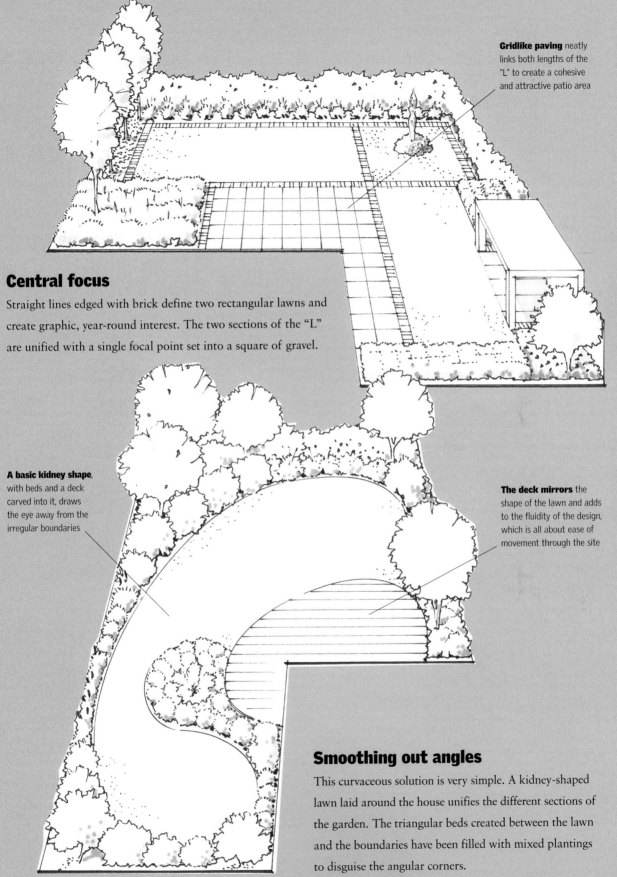

Gridlike paving neatly links both lengths of the "L" to create a cohesive and attractive patio area

Central focus

Straight lines edged with brick define two rectangular lawns and create graphic, year-round interest. The two sections of the "L" are unified with a single focal point set into a square of gravel.

A basic kidney shape, with beds and a deck carved into it, draws the eye away from the irregular boundaries

The deck mirrors the shape of the lawn and adds to the fluidity of the design, which is all about ease of movement through the site

Smoothing out angles

This curvaceous solution is very simple. A kidney-shaped lawn laid around the house unifies the different sections of the garden. The triangular beds created between the lawn and the boundaries have been filled with mixed plantings to disguise the angular corners.

87

Corner and irregularly-shaped yards

Irregularly-shaped yards are often the most fun to work with; it's a really great challenge to be faced with something that isn't a perfect rectangle. Avoid focusing on the boundaries by creating interest toward the center of the space, and keep your design simple. Determine where you want your visitors to go, and where the eye should look, by using directional lines and shapes, and creating points of interest with planting and hard landscaping.

Oval sweep

The design for this five-cornered garden is based around an oval-shaped lawn in the center. This opens up the space, while the areas of planting help to disguise the inhospitable boundaries.

A pavilion has been placed in the deepest border. Slightly off-center, it's a great device for directing the eye

An island bed creates interest and a sense of mystery by obscuring the space behind it

All squared up

With its acute angles, this corner garden presents a very particular problem. Here, the lawn and gravel areas create an essentially square central space, while beds hug the hard landscaping, deflecting the focus away from the awkward triangles.

Decking and an area of gravel lead out onto the L-shaped lawn

This acute angle, like the one diagonally opposite, has been partly disguised with mass planting

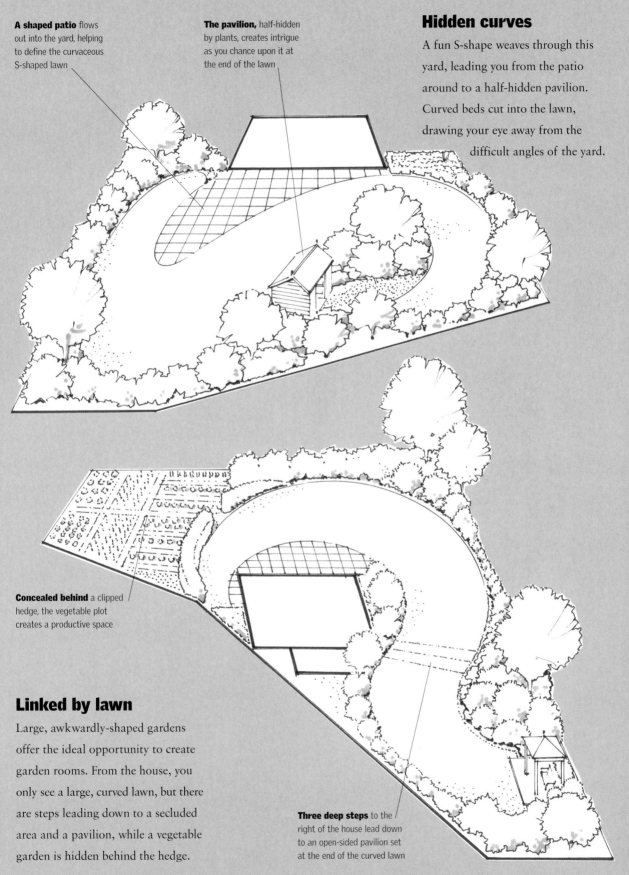

A shaped patio flows
out into the yard, helping
to define the curvaceous
S-shaped lawn

The pavilion, half-hidden
by plants, creates intrigue
as you chance upon it at
the end of the lawn

Hidden curves

A fun S-shape weaves through this
yard, leading you from the patio
around to a half-hidden pavilion.
Curved beds cut into the lawn,
drawing your eye away from the
difficult angles of the yard.

Concealed behind a clipped
hedge, the vegetable plot
creates a productive space

Linked by lawn

Large, awkwardly-shaped gardens
offer the ideal opportunity to create
garden rooms. From the house, you
only see a large, curved lawn, but there
are steps leading down to a secluded
area and a pavilion, while a vegetable
garden is hidden behind the hedge.

Three deep steps to the
right of the house lead down
to an open-sided pavilion set
at the end of the curved lawn

5
Balance & proportion

You always know when you're entering a balanced, well-proportioned garden because it feels comfortable—lines lead you naturally through the space, and shapes and volumes are restful to the eye. Some contemporary designers purposely set out to create slight discord by building gardens that are off-balance, but most of us want our outdoor spaces to **offer a peaceful sanctuary**. So, how do you achieve balance and proportion?

First, think about your garden in proportion to the human body. A tall hedge planted close to the house may appear too dominant as you enter the garden, but when set at the far end of the site, the **perspective makes it seem more apt** and less formidable. Flowerbeds dotted around the garden look unbalanced and chaotic if they have not been set out to follow a line (*see Chapter 4*). They make you feel like you're in a messy room, while broad, flowing borders that sweep gracefully through the space, or wide, straight flowerbeds flanking a pool, **create order** and immediately relax you.

Treat your garden like a room in your house: there, you know instinctively when you mark out an area for a new sofa whether it will look right in the space. Do the same outside. Measure and mark out the position of your planned features with sand from a bottle, a spray marker, or canes, to see how they fit. Or **take photos and draw features** and plantings on them to check the sizes and proportions. You don't need to draw accurate representations; simple, blocky shapes will give you an idea of how they will look *in situ*.

Achieving balance is easier in formal gardens because they are set out in a symmetrical pattern (*opposite*), but informal designs have to be judged more by eye. To help you design a **well-balanced and well-proportioned** garden, I've looked at examples of poorly designed yards, and shown how they can be recrafted to create more comfortable spaces.

A balanced, well-proportioned garden feels comfortable—lines lead you naturally through the space, and the shapes are restful to the eye

Defining the space

The various elements in this large, open yard stand completely separate from each other, giving the impression that you're in a huge landscape where space is no object. The house is surrounded by almost uninterrupted lawn, and the lot's main features comprise a cherry tree, a driveway, and a fence, with a few small, skimpy beds planted around the building. The site has some appeal, but it's hardly inviting. The isolated elements need to be brought together, given cohesion, and the house and garden must be linked. The massive lawn also needs better definition to make the yard feel more restful and balanced, like a green carpet.

Isolated features *Each of the elements here is isolated, and they need to be brought together to create a more unified, interesting design.*

The pretty cherry tree remains the dominant focal point, but the borders now link it with the house

Sweeping borders create a better balance between the house and garden

The lawn is reshaped to form a dynamic swirl, and provides a stage set on which the tree performs as a stunning focal point

Cohesive curves

Enlarging the small beds into one sweeping border unifies the disparate elements. It swoops around the cherry tree, integrating it into the design, and is filled with a mix of shrubs, small trees, and perennials. The planting focuses attention away from the driveway, which originally looked rather harsh, and the house and yard are now more balanced.

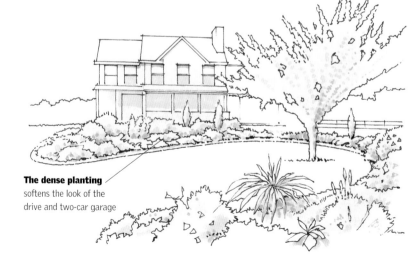

The dense planting softens the look of the drive and two-car garage

Framing the house

This is a quite pretty piece of architecture in an urban setting. The garden should be doing more to show off the simple, red brick house with its attractive windows and interesting details around the door. The yard is uninviting—a straight concrete path presents everything to you right away, and offers no sense of intrigue. Your eye is also drawn to the houses behind by the awkward arrangement of garages that are visible around the back. A more appealing design is needed here. The new garden must still offer enough space to park a car or two, but it should have a more welcoming feel, develop a sense of privacy, and frame the house.

Obvious offerings *There is no mystery or intrigue in this garden: a concrete driveway leads straight past a plain lawn to the front door.*

Tall, slim trees shield the front of the house from the street, yet cast very little shade on the property

A curved drive maximizes the use of space, and focuses the eye on the lush planting

The door is framed with a porch built from the same materials as the arbor

A secret garden

Privacy and a sense of suspense are delivered with this new design. The concrete is replaced with a curved, cobbled driveway edged with lush planting, which also frames the windows. The arbor draws the eye into the garden and hides the front door, thereby increasing privacy.

The arbor frames the house and emphasizes its attractive features

The cobbled drive has a warmth and texture that invite you into the property

95

Balancing the landscape

There's something a bit awkward and unbalanced about this lush and well-kept garden. The owner obviously loves gardening and spending time in the greenhouse, since the main path runs straight to the glass structure. In terms of design, the yard clearly belongs to someone who likes a degree of formality, but there's no resolution here—the lawn is ill-defined and the small birdbath looks slightly incongruous at the end of the path. With these clues, I have an immediate idea about the garden style the owner would like, which has led me to create a semiformal design with more balanced rectangular lawns enclosed by lots of plants. The birdbath is used as the focus at the center of the far lawn.

Beauty without unity *This yard needs a design to balance the features and provide focus.*

The birdbath, which looked a bit lost at the end of the curved path, is used more confidently as a focal point in the center of the lawn

Two rectangular lawns create symmetry and balance, and are better proportioned than a single expanse of grass

Dividing the yard in two

I've introduced balance by dividing the yard and formalizing the design. Geometric shapes and straight lines create order, and the planting is given more prominence in the center of the yard, and in the straight borders.

The line of the path is softened by breaking it up into stepping stones

Lollipop-shaped trees separate the lawns, and play up the formal theme

Creating formality

This old-fashioned garden has much appeal, but it needs reinventing to create better-proportioned spaces using simple, geometric shapes. The yard looks as though it could be situated at the edge of a woodland. The beds are filled with shrubs that were popular from the late '60s until recently, and the island bed is dotted with stones that look as if they have been removed from a rockery. My plan is to formalize the design to take greater advantage of the background planting, and to build a garden room, from which plants and wildlife can be enjoyed whatever the season.

Old-fashioned style *The planting in this garden creates a beautiful backdrop, but the wavy borders and irregular-shaped beds need to be redrawn to provide greater clarity.*

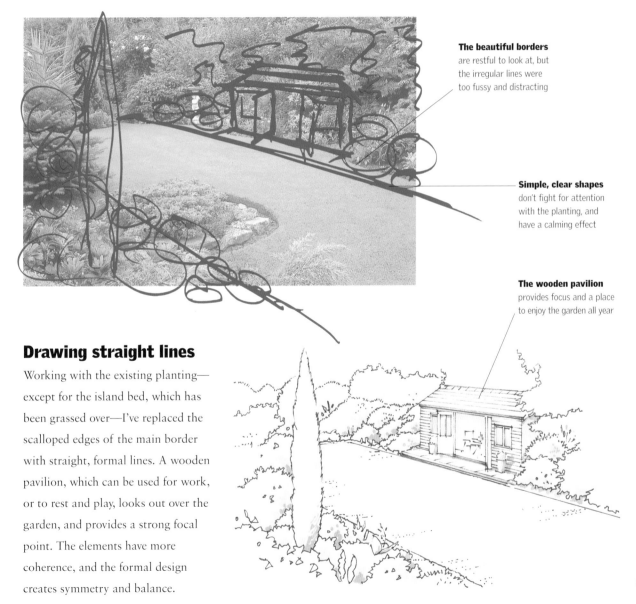

The beautiful borders are restful to look at, but the irregular lines were too fussy and distracting

Simple, clear shapes don't fight for attention with the planting, and have a calming effect

The wooden pavilion provides focus and a place to enjoy the garden all year

Drawing straight lines

Working with the existing planting— except for the island bed, which has been grassed over—I've replaced the scalloped edges of the main border with straight, formal lines. A wooden pavilion, which can be used for work, or to rest and play, looks out over the garden, and provides a strong focal point. The elements have more coherence, and the formal design creates symmetry and balance.

Smoothing out lines

Complicated and too busy, this yard needs updating and a bit of tidying up. The zigzag concrete path brutally separates the elements in the garden, and the rockery is full of miniature conifers in too many shades of lime green. Unbalanced and poorly proportioned, the overall impression is of a surreal mess. It has its good points, though, and is nicely enclosed with dense planting that provides a strong backdrop.

Zigzag path *A line of concrete divides the garden, with beds dotted on either side that look messy and haphazard.*

The hedge is a real asset, creating a smooth, organic green wall around the garden, and offering a sense of privacy

A stepping stone path flows through the garden, linking the oval lawns

The greenhouse has been left in place but softened with more plantings

Dynamic shapes

I have given the garden direction by setting it on diagonal lines, and linked two oval lawns with a pathway that follows the curve of the shapes. The rockery and sporadic planting have been replaced with more defined beds, and the tree that stood alone in a circular bed is now integrated into the larger border by the greenhouse. The design looks balanced and there are more usable spaces, while the features are better proportioned.

The lawns and beds are in perfect balance so that neither detracts from the other

Harmonizing the elements

With its blobby and kidney-shaped beds scattered across a large area of lawn, and dramatically scalloped borders, this is almost a Regency-style garden. The design has no coherence: you're not led in any particular direction, your eye has nothing to focus on, and even the planting in the background lacks potential. It looks as though the yard has been built up in layers over time, with no eye on the overall look—this is a garden where the big picture (*see Chapter 3*) has not been considered. The solution is to create harmony by linking together the separate elements.

Scattered details   *Small island beds filled with plants and rocks have been placed at random, creating a rather chaotic design.*

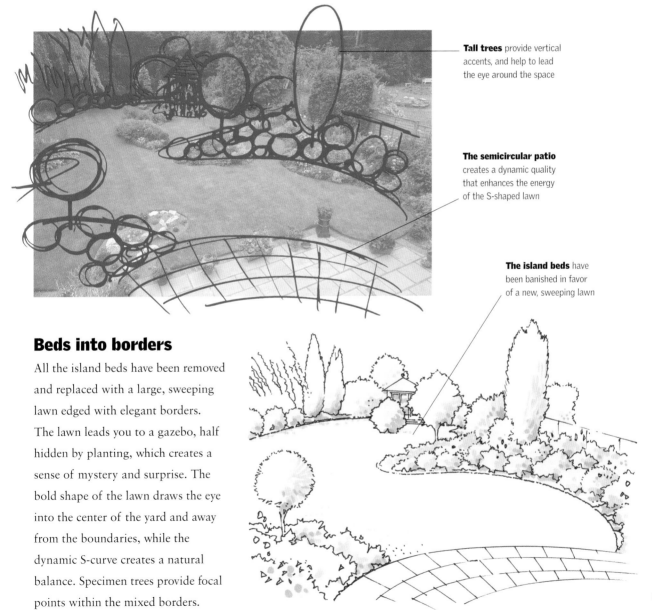

Tall trees provide vertical accents, and help to lead the eye around the space

The semicircular patio creates a dynamic quality that enhances the energy of the S-shaped lawn

The island beds have been banished in favor of a new, sweeping lawn

Beds into borders

All the island beds have been removed and replaced with a large, sweeping lawn edged with elegant borders. The lawn leads you to a gazebo, half hidden by planting, which creates a sense of mystery and surprise. The bold shape of the lawn draws the eye into the center of the yard and away from the boundaries, while the dynamic S-curve creates a natural balance. Specimen trees provide focal points within the mixed borders.

Introducing privacy

Urban life means living in close proximity to other properties, making privacy in the backyard a priority for many. We want to look out from our windows onto a leafy scene—not other people's bricks and mortar—and relax outside in relative seclusion. This yard is typical of many newer urban housing developments, where angular concrete paving dominates. Although it contains some nice plants, the design just doesn't work. The overall impression is not friendly or inviting, and the planting designed to help screen the garden from neighbors has not been used strategically.

Exposed patio *This garden is crying out for taller planting to block the view of the patio area from the houses beyond the boundaries.*

The square pool has been retained and set into the deck to create a focal point

To soften the look of the garden, a wooden deck has replaced the original concrete paving

A large tree screens the patio from the neighbors' windows

Planting screens

In the redesigned garden, the concrete has been replaced with a softer wooden deck. I've also extended the lawn into the line of the old patio to create a more interesting shape, and reworked the boundary planting to include taller trees to screen the yard from the buildings behind. There is now a better balance between the deck, lawn, and borders.

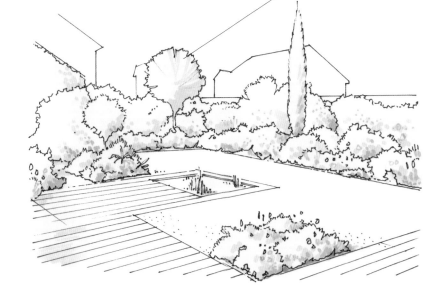

Increasing proportions

Focal points are an important part of a successful garden design. They direct the eye and add instant drama, but to do so they have to be of the right size to make a statement. In this garden, the focal point is a terracotta urn set in front of a beautifully clipped hedge, but because it's so tiny in relation to the space, it leaves you with a feeling of anticlimax. The owners of this garden obviously like formality, and I think it's also in need of something over-the-top, and maybe a bit humorous.

Tiny detail *The urn used as a focal point here is proportionally too small for a garden of this size.*

The Indian-style temple and seat are fun, yet formal, and hint at exotic Eastern architecture

A rectangular pool stretches out in front of the temple, reflecting its elegant shape and form

Italian cypresses are used to add height and frame the temple, giving it extra prominence

Eastern inspirations

The main feature in the new design is an Indian-inspired temple, flanked by two Italian cypress trees, and mirrored in a rectangular pool. The pool also creates a great sense of perspective as the eye travels along it to the temple at the end. Two spheres clipped into the hedge frame the scene. Features are balanced and in proportion to the size and scale of the yard.

6

What have you got?

Now that you've worked out your needs, looked at styles you like, and learned a bit about general design principles, it's time to take stock of what you've got to work with. So, before going any further, **take a good look at your yard**. Your discoveries will help you to create a design that really works, both on an aesthetic level and as a practical, functional space.

The process of assessing your site is the same, whether you're redesigning a garden that has been nurtured over a long period, upgrading an established site that you have recently purchased, or creating a design for a newly built home.

The first stage is to **look at what your yard offers** in its present state. Is it sunny and warm, and ideal for a terrace or patio, or is it in shade for most of the day? A shady garden needs more careful scrutiny to see when and where sun falls throughout the day; if you have the patience, take notes in both summer and winter, when the sun is lower in the sky. This information tells you where to **site your patios** and seating areas, and what type of plants will thrive in your garden.

If your plants are to flourish, you must also get to know your soil. The yards of **new properties** will probably have been landscaped by the developer, and although you can't expect the design to be of the highest quality, it may have a veneer of beauty. But the soil is unlikely to be in a healthy state—in many cases, construction rubble is buried just below the surface, and the topsoil may have been compacted by machinery.

Another important consideration is the topography of your yard—is it a hilly, windy site, or a low-lying frost pocket? **Do you have a wonderful view** that can be integrated into your garden design, or is your yard overlooked, or marred by an eyesore? Take time to assess all of these factors before you start measuring up your garden for the scale plan.

Your discoveries about your yard will help you create a design that works, both on an aesthetic level and as a practical, functional space

Garden exposure

Observing the exposure is usually my first task when visiting a new site. Exposure simply means the direction in which the garden is facing, and you can determine yours with the aid of a simple compass, or by noting where the sun is at different times of the day. The fact that the sun rises in the east and sets in the west should demonstrate which way your yard faces.

Sunlight is important because, in general, we like to look out on a bright, sunny garden. From the house it becomes a well-lit picture, drawing us out to explore its unfolding stories. The sun makes us feel warm and healthy, too, but the searing heat of a south-facing garden in summer can be oppressive, and you will need to plan areas of shade to create comfortable oases. In yards that face north, seek out the sun at the end of your garden and design seating areas that soak up the precious rays.

In the plant world, many species we love need a sunny site, but don't despair if your garden only gets sun for part of the day, or is mostly in shade, since there are plenty of plants that have evolved to flourish in these conditions.

Facing the sun *To determine the exposure of your yard, stand with your back to the house: you are now looking in the direction your garden faces.*

South-facing gardens

Gardens that face south are very desirable in cooler climates, since they receive the sun all day, and are light and bright. This can be a real bonus in spring and fall when you want to make the most of every warm day, but in the height of summer, a south-facing garden can be unbearably hot. Counter the heat by including shaded areas, using either tall plantings or, for instant results, pergolas, arbors, walls, and screens.

North-facing gardens

Sunlight is in short supply in a north-facing garden, and in winter you may get no sun at all. The problem is not so bad in long gardens, since the far end will be sunny because it is beyond the shadow made by the house. In small yards, avoid tall boundaries that cast even more shade; also take note of where the sun falls throughout the day and use these areas for seating.

East-facing gardens

Breakfasting alfresco is one of the joys of life, and on an east-facing patio, sheltered by the house, you can take full advantage of the early-morning sun. Evenings are cool, however, so find a spot for a seat at the far end of the garden that traps the last rays of sun. Also, avoid growing plants that are susceptible to frost damage, such as camellias, in direct morning sun.

West-facing gardens

You'll have to find an area at the end of a west-facing garden to drink your morning coffee, but afternoons and evenings will be warm and sunny. A garden that faces west is perfect for party animals, with plenty of scope for a dance floor or dining area drenched in warm evening light. Morning shade is also good for those feeling delicate the day after!

Hills and valleys

Those living on top of a hill know that it can be pretty blustery up there. Wind can damage plants and make gardens cold and inhospitable, so it is vital to protect your yard with sturdy windbreaks.

Although valleys are sheltered from wind, they are often colder than hilltops. This is because frost travels downhill and settles in valleys, lowering temperatures.

Windswept hilltops *These trees clearly demonstrate the effects of wind damage. To protect exposed gardens, construct windbreaks around your property. Deciduous hedges are ideal, or fences with an open construction that allow about 50 percent of the air to pass through.*

Frost pockets *Gardens in valleys are often cold and suffer more frosts than those farther up the hillside. Reduce frost damage by putting up solid barriers, such as walls or hedging, on the uphill slope. These will trap cold air behind them, keeping your garden frost-free.*

Climate considerations

As well as looking at the direction your garden faces, consider your local climate. The levels of rain, frost, and snow your garden experiences will affect your choice of plants and how much shelter you require. Also, find out your area's temperature extremes, because each plant species has a maximum and minimum at which it can survive.

I live near the coast in Ireland, which has a maritime climate influenced by warm air from the Gulf Stream. The surrounding seas stabilize temperatures and increase rainfall, and because there are few frosts, some plants from warmer climates grow happily here.

Microclimates Local conditions are influenced by the national climate, but this is often only half the picture. There are other factors that can make your particular garden warmer or colder than your neighbor's yard, and wetter or drier than those in a nearby town.

For example, temperatures may be lower in gardens attached to properties that are divided by an alley or passageway, where wind is forced through the gap to form a wind tunnel. A patio at the end of the tunnel will be uncomfortably cold, and delicate or tall plants could also suffer. To combat this problem, construct a windbreak (*see left*) in the path of the tunnel, and site your seating areas in a more sheltered spot.

Gardens shaded by a neighbor's garage or tall buildings and those at the bottom of a hill where frost collects (*see left*) will also experience lower temperatures than adjacent properties.

A patio at the end of a wind tunnel will be cold and uncomfortable

Buried utility supplies To avoid fines or repair bills—and possibly serious injuries—you should always check the location of gas pipes, sewer lines, and electric, phone, and television cables before you start digging or building, especially if you're working in the front yard, where buried utilities are commonly found. In many areas, you are required by law to call your local utility companies or a public utility locating service at least 48 hours before you begin work, so that buried cables or pipes can be pinpointed with special detectors and flagged.

Rain gutters Consider the location of your downspouts when planning a garden, since runoff from frequent rains can drown delicate plants and wash away soil. You could create a "rain garden" of moisture-loving plants to soak up the water—and help the environment by keeping stormwater out of sewers, lakes, and rivers.

Boundaries and special features

When surveying your site, take special note of the boundaries, and the view beyond them. Hedges make wonderful natural backdrops to planting plans, create windbreaks, and offer homes for birds and wildlife, so I always think twice before removing one.

Decide what features you want to keep, and those you can live without. I'm more ruthless with built structures, such as sheds, than with mature trees and plants, even if they're in the wrong place. I figure that trees take years to grow and offer unsurpassed beauty.

View to hide *If your yard is overlooked, a wall or screen can be used to mask the neighbors' view of your space. Create private seating or dining areas behind the screen, or beneath a covered arbor.*

View to embrace *Those lucky enough to enjoy a spectacular view should try to integrate it into their design. Use plantings along boundaries, rather than fences, to blend the garden into the landscape beyond.*

Understanding your soil

Getting to know your soil is an essential part of the design process. The type of soil you have in your garden determines how well it retains water and nutrients, how easy it is to dig, and the type of plants that thrive in it.

The arrangement of particles in the soil is known as its "structure." Sandy soils are made up of relatively large particles that leave big gaps, or pores, between them, while clay soils comprise tiny particles separated by minute spaces. It is not the size of the particles but the size of the spaces that determines how well or badly the soil retains water and nutrients. For example, sandy soils are free-draining because the large gaps between the particles allow water to flow through quickly. And because plant nutrients are dissolved in water, sandy soils can be less fertile.

The tiny pores between clay particles trap and hold water and nutrients. The downside is that clay soils become waterlogged very quickly, and the particles pack together in wet conditions when the soil is compressed, squeezing out the oxygen essential for plant growth. Walking on wet clay will further compact the soil.

Most garden soils are made up of not just one type of soil but a mixture. The best soil is moist but well-drained, fertile, and easy to dig!

What type of soil do you have?

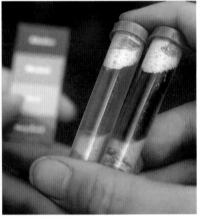

Sandy soil When rubbed between your fingers, sandy soil feels gritty and falls apart if you try to roll it into a ball. Coarse sand is free-draining, but very fine sand doesn't drain well and can easily become compacted. Sandy soils are low in nutrients but easy to dig, which is why they are known as "light soils."

Clay soil This type of soil feels smooth and sticky, and can be rolled into a ball when wet. Clay is also porous and holds nutrients and water well, although plants cannot extract all of the moisture from clay, because an electrical charge on each of the particles holds it too tightly—rather like iron filings clinging to a magnet.

Acidity and alkalinity Some plants, such as azaleas, only grow well on acidic soils, while others, such as acanthus, prefer alkaline conditions, so it is important to establish the pH (acidity or alkalinity) of your soil. Soil testing kits are available and easy to use. Take a few soil samples—the pH may differ throughout your yard.

Sandy soil feels gritty when rubbed between your fingers, while clay soils have a smooth, sticky texture

Improving your soil

The good news is that whatever type of soil you have, it can be improved.

Organic matter (*top left*) All soils benefit from the addition of organic matter, that magical cure-all for poor soil conditions. Organic matter, such as garden compost or farmyard manure, is gradually decomposed by microorganisms to form "humus," a black substance that improves the structure of your soil. When mixed with sandy soil, humus helps to fill the gaps between the particles, thereby increasing its nutrient- and water-holding capacity. It also bonds tiny clay particles into larger "crumbs," which increases the size of the spaces between them, improving drainage and reducing waterlogging. Organic matter acts as a slow-release plant fertilizer as well, giving you two benefits for the price of one. Dig it into sandy soils in the spring and clay soils in the fall.

Mulching (*left*) You can also use organic matter as a mulch. Spread a thick layer, about 2 in (5 cm) deep, over your soil after it has rained or you have watered it. The mulch helps stop water from evaporating from the soil surface. As the season progresses, worms and other soil creatures gradually take it below the surface where it feeds the plants' roots.

Adding sand (*below left*) Dig in sand or pea gravel if your soil is prone to waterlogging. A wheelbarrowful per square yard (meter) will help to open up heavy clay and increase drainage.

Measuring equipment

As well as pencils and a large sketchbook or large sheet of paper, you'll need tape measures of various sizes—small metal measures are perfect for hard-to-reach places, while medium and extra-long tape measures are handy for large gardens. You will also need string and pegs or stakes, a level for measuring gradients, and a friend to help you.

Long level
Used to measure gradients (*see p114*).

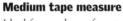

Small metal tape measure
These are useful for areas that are difficult to access, because the metal tape remains rigid.

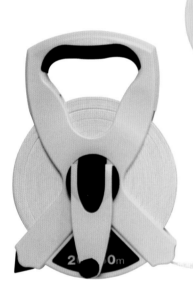

Medium tape measure
Ideal for gardens of up to 100 ft (30 m), but not as cumbersome as an extra-long tape measure.

Extra-long tape measure
Perfect for distances up to 200 ft (60 m). When taking readings, make sure your tape measure, whatever its length, is taut and straight.

Pegs and string
To mark out a perfectly straight line between two points, use special plastic pegs with string attached, or a length of string tied to two stakes. Pull the string taut to make an accurate line.

Giant tri-square
This huge square is used to check right angles, and is needed to plot offsets (*see p115*).

Measuring your yard

You need to measure your yard to create a scale plan (*see pp116-7*), but the method you choose depends on the shape of your lot. Use a simple technique (*see below and right*) for regular square or rectangular yards, or more advanced methods (*see pp114-5*) if your yard is an irregular shape or you need a more accurate plan.

Before you measure up, draw a rough sketch of your garden. I tend to do this from an upstairs window where I can get a clear view, but if this is not possible, examine the garden from both ends. It really doesn't matter at this stage if your rough plan is not perfect. I use a large sketchbook for this job, because it offers sufficient space for the plan and notes, but isn't too awkward to haul around. Your outline sketch should include boundaries, as well as main features, such as patios, paths, steps, garages, pools, flowerbeds, and any prominent planting.

On a separate piece of paper, jot down the features you plan to keep, and those you want to lose. As you walk around your garden, take note of anything that needs maintenance or repairs.

Simple measuring techniques You don't need to measure your garden too precisely if you have an even-sided yard and plan to keep the interest in the center, with planting around the edges. Here, measure the house (noting the position of the windows and doors), boundaries, diagonals from each corner, and the position of features (*see right*). The two diagonal measurements should be of equal length if the sides of the yard are equal.

> *On a piece of paper, jot down the features you plan to keep, and those you want to lose*

Measuring a rectangular yard

If your yard is a straight-sided rectangle or square, simply measure all of the boundaries and the two diagonals, plus the position of your features. Use these measurements to make a simple scale plan (*see p116*).

1

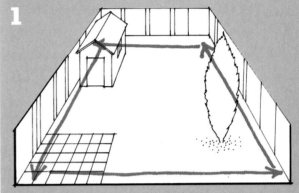

Boundaries *Carefully measure all four sides of your yard, noting them clearly on your rough sketch.*

2

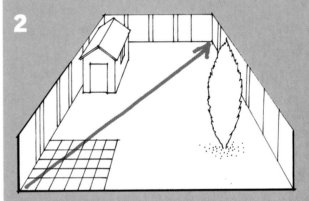

Diagonals *Measure diagonally across the yard from corner to corner. Repeat for the opposite diagonal.*

3

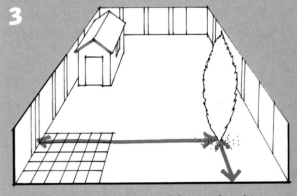

Features *Plot large plants and features by taking measurements at 90° from the house and a boundary.*

113

Advanced measuring techniques There are two suitable methods of measuring irregularly shaped yards: "triangulation," and "taking offsets." Both methods enable you to plot the exact position of boundaries and features, which can then be plotted on a scale plan (*see p117*).

Triangulation involves measuring a line from a point on the property to a boundary or feature. You then measure from a different point on the house to the same point on the boundary or feature. When these lines are drawn onto your rough sketch they form a triangle, hence the term triangulation (*see right*).

To take offsets, lay a long tape measure at 90° from the house to the end of the garden. Then take measurements at right angles from this line to the boundaries or features (*see right*).

Measuring the gradient of a sloping garden is important where the site is to be terraced (*see below*). If your garden is on a slope with a very steep gradient and you plan large-scale earth-moving or decked terraces, it may be best to employ a professional surveyor to chart the site.

Draw a scale plan When you have taken all the measurements you need, transfer them onto a scale plan (*see pp116-7*). The scale you use depends on the size of your garden. In general, for a medium to large garden, use a scale of ⅛":1' (or 1:100 cm); ¼":1' (or 1:50 cm) for small gardens; and ½":1' (or 1:20 cm) for courtyards or patio areas.

When you have taken all the measurements you need, transfer them onto a scale plan

Measuring gradients

You will need:

1 length of wood just over 3 ft (1 m) long
Level and tape measure
3 or 4 pegs on which to lay the plank of wood

1 Hammer in a peg level with the soil at the top of the slope, and hammer in a second peg 3 ft (1 m) farther down the slope. Lay the wood on the pegs and, using a level, adjust the lower peg until the wood is level.
2 Remove the wood, and measure the height of the second peg from ground level. This tells you the "fall" over 3 ft (1 m).
3 Leave the second peg where it is but hammer it in level with the ground. Hammer a third peg 3 ft (1 m) farther down the slope, lay the wood on top, and again adjust the height of

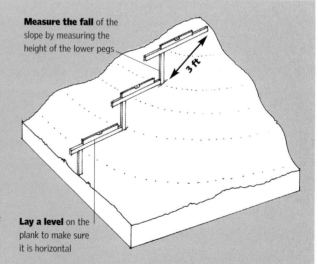

Measure the fall of the slope by measuring the height of the lower pegs

3 ft

Lay a level on the plank to make sure it is horizontal

this lower peg until the wood is sitting level. Then measure the peg, as you did in Step 2.
4 Repeat Step 3 until you have measured the whole slope. To calculate the fall, add up your measurements. In the example above, the 9-ft slope has a fall of 3 ft (12 in + 10 in +14 in).

Triangulation and offsets

Select only one method of measurement, and stick to this to avoid confusion. Measuring is much easier with two people, especially if you have a medium-sized or large yard, so try to enlist a friend to help you.

Whether using triangulation or taking offsets, take measurements of the facade of your house, and any gaps between the building and boundary.

To plot a curved or uneven boundary using triangulation, take measurements at about 3-ft (1-m) intervals. Draw the triangles and note the measurements you make on your rough sketch.

When taking offsets, use a giant tri-square (*see p112*) to ensure that your tape measure is at exactly 90° to the house, and that the second tape is at right angles to the first (*see below right*). If these angles are slightly out, your plan will not be accurate. Mark each of your measurements onto your rough sketch.

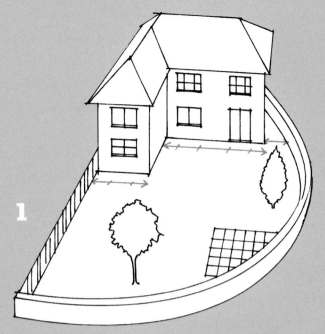

Measure the house Take a series of measurements across the facade of the house, noting the position of doors, windows, and bays. Also note the distance from the side of the house to the boundary. Mark all of these measurements clearly on your rough sketch.

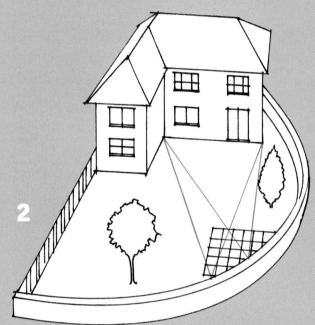

Triangulation Measure from one corner of the house to a point on the boundary, or a feature, such as a tree. Repeat from another point on the house to the same point on the boundary or feature. Note these on your sketch.

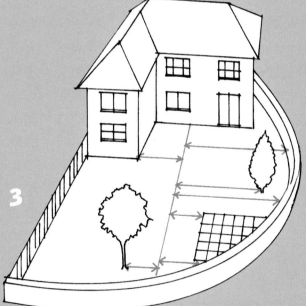

Taking offsets Peg a tape measure at 90° to the house at a point you measured in Step 1 (*above*), and lay it along the length of the garden. Lay a second tape at 90° to the first to measure the position of boundaries and features.

Drawing up a scale plan for a square or rectangular yard

When you have decided what scale you are going to use (*see p114*), convert all your measurements and make a note of them. Professional designers generally draw plans on a drawing board, but if you don't have one, use graph paper. Or, if you have a computer, buy garden design software and enter the measurements into the program.

You will need:

Graph paper (or plain paper and T-square)

Clear plastic ruler

Pencil, eraser, and pen for final plan

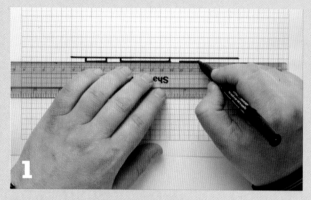

1

Draw the house doors and windows Start at the bottom left-hand corner of your page and draw on the house wall, showing the position of doors and windows.

2

Position the boundaries If your yard is either square or rectangular, draw to scale the left- and right-hand boundaries at 90° to the house wall, and connect them.

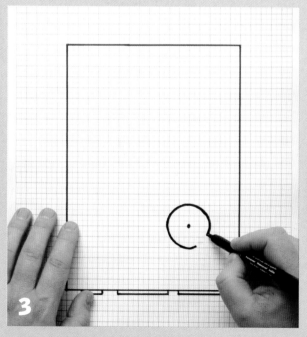

3

Add trees and major plantings Using the measurements you took from the house and boundaries (*see p113*), draw on trees and large plants, including their canopies.

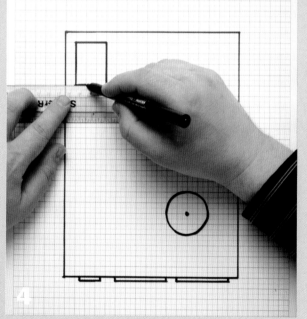

4

Plot all other features Carefully draw on patios, pools, paths, garages, and outbuildings, regardless of whether you intend to keep them.

Drawing up a scale plan for an irregularly shaped yard

Use the method below if you used triangulation to plot boundaries and features (*see p115*). If you took offsets, transfer measurements onto a scale plan. Draw on the house, a line representing the tape at 90° to it, and boundaries and features at 90° to this line (*see p115*).

You will need:

Graph paper

Ruler, pencil, eraser, and pen

Large compass

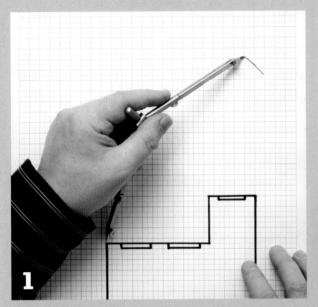

1

Make first arc Draw the house. Set the compass to the first measurement you took from the house. Put the point where you measured from on the house, and draw an arc.

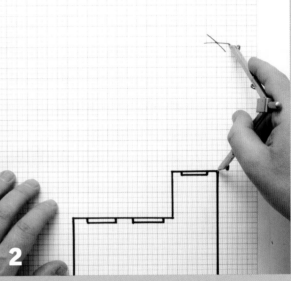

2

Draw second arc Reset the compass to the second measurement. Put the point where you measured from on the house, and draw a second arc to cross the first.

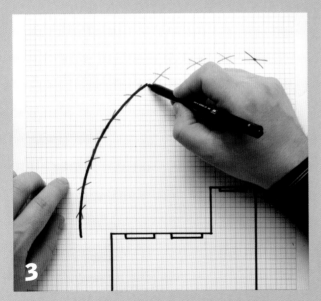

3

Connect the dots Repeat Steps 1 and 2 for all of your boundary triangulation measurements. Connect the center points of each of the crosses to plot your boundary.

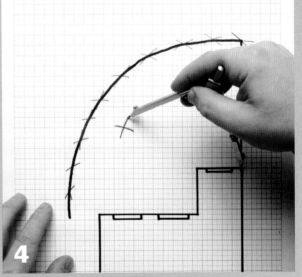

4

Add the details Using the same technique outlined in Steps 1 to 3, plot the position of buildings, trees, plants, and other major features to create your scale plan.

7

Planning your design

To create a good garden design, you don't have to draw a plan, but it can help. Some people are able to **assess their space instinctively** without committing anything to paper. They have the confidence to decide what they want, lay down lines, create the shape, and design the planting. For others, drawing a plan is a necessary exercise. Sketching out your designs forces you to **consider all your options**, and allows you to work on numerous possibilities for your yard. It doesn't restrict you—you can adapt your designs at any time before construction—but it's good to visualize the essence of your garden, so that you can consider **the benefits and the pitfalls** before you commit to its implementation.

Putting pen to paper may scare you, especially if you feel you can't draw, but everyone can—it just takes practice. First, take your scale plan and either photocopy it several times or draw on a tracing-paper overlay. Alternatively, use a computer garden design program to draw up your ideas. Then go back to your **list of wants, needs, and styles** outlined in Chapters 1 and 2. I take lots of photos of the yard and spread them out on the table in front of me to remind me of the different areas. You can then draw features on tracing paper laid over your photos to give you an idea of how they will look *in situ*. When you have something you like, transfer your ideas onto your paper plan.

A plan can also give you an idea of **the costs involved and the materials** you will need. You shouldn't restrict your dreams, but you should be aware of the budget, and the time scale, both for completing the building work and for your planting to mature.

You won't always get your design right the first time, but the process of laying down your ideas will **lead you in the right direction**. In this chapter, I have designed three gardens to show how to develop a successful plan, and how the final designs evolved.

The design plan forces you to consider all your options, and allows you to work on the numerous possibilities for your yard

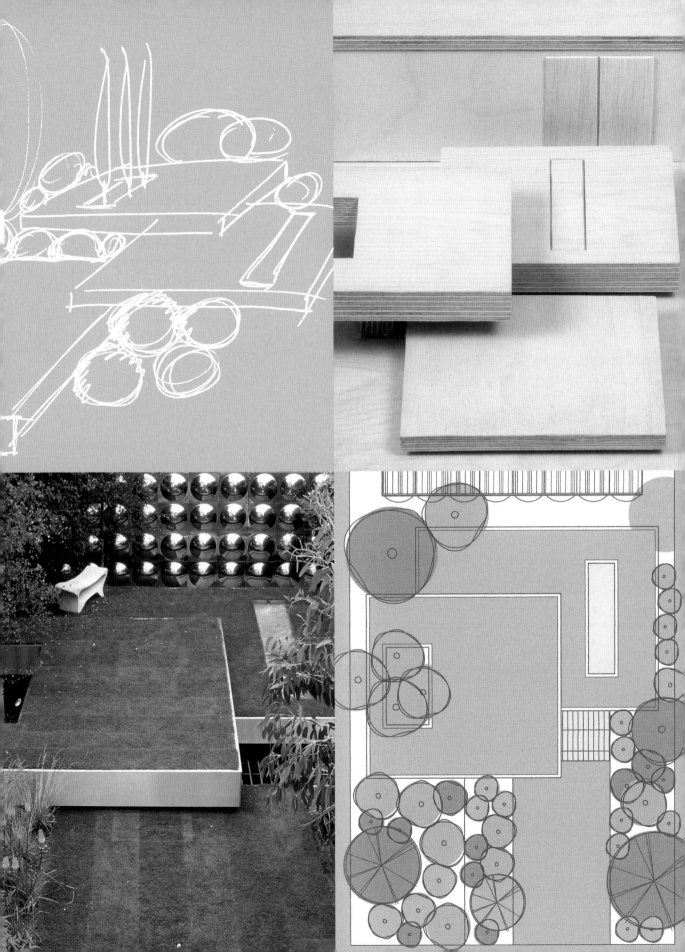

Designs for a rectangular garden

The first plan is for a thin, rectangular yard, owned by a young urban couple looking for a relaxing space where they can dine and entertain friends. The original site included a beautiful cherry tree halfway down the garden, with a paved area opposite. While the patio was disposable, the tree needed more consideration. Removing it would open up the view, but I liked the way it divided part of the garden. There was also a shed, which was to be retained, at the end of the garden. Clearly visible from the house, it was too dominant in that position, and would have to be moved to a more suitable location.

Garden format

Size   80 ft x 30 ft (25 m x 10 m)
Owners Young couple, no children
Aspect South-facing
View   Overlooked at back by tall houses

Wants and needs

• A place to wine, dine, and entertain friends
• Privacy from neighboring properties
• A shed to house lawnmower and other tools
• Somewhere to sunbathe, read, and relax
• A stylish, contemporary look
• Low maintenance, easy-to-care-for planting

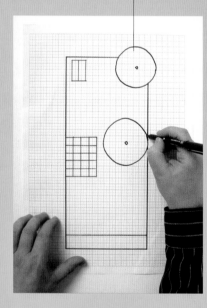

Two mature trees, a cherry in the center of the yard, and a laburnum at the end, added natural beauty to the yard, and I wanted to keep them

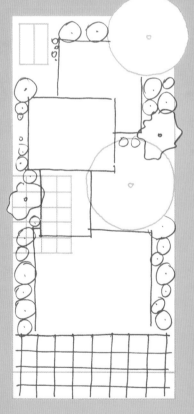

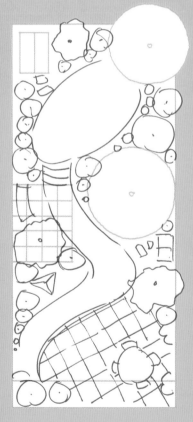

The scale plan

Before you start to design, measure your site and draw a scale plan (*see Chapter 6*). Here, the plan shows how isolated the patio by the fence looks.

First thoughts

My original sketches are based on squares and rectangles, with a patio close to the house; but they are too angular and rigid.

Introducing curves

The next plan includes curves, with a winding path leading down to an oval lawn. It fits the brief but doesn't use the space very well.

Final design

The third sketch is almost there; however, the shape at the end was too awkward. Instead of the path running straight to a new curve, I have created a raised circular lawn separated by brick steps from a grass walkway. The deck by the house mirrors the fluid shapes, and both trees have been retained.

Brick steps link the path with the circular lawn; the same bricks are used for a mowing edge

A topiary bay tree clipped into a standard forms an elegant focal point in the lawn

The cherry tree marks the end of the lawn path, and offers a shady area beneath for ferns

The shed hidden beneath the cherry and masked by new planting is less obvious

The furniture comprises a round table and chairs in a modern style

Working up ideas

Building on the last sketch, I have opened up the curved path, which winds around the cherry that restricts the view of the end of the yard.

The clothesline is easy to access from the house, and because it collapses it is much less visible when not in use

An oval deck mirrors the swooping curves in the rest of the garden. The wooden surface has a warm look and feels soft under foot

Plans for a large garden with a sea view

The family that owns this cottage-style property set within a large square yard is looking to make the most of the wraparound garden. The relatively shallow back garden has its limitations, but, fortunately, the eye travels over the boundaries to the spectacular coastal view beyond. The difficulty for me was how to make the space into a comfortable garden and "plant" the house into its surroundings.

Garden format

Size 100 ft x 80 ft (30 m x 25 m)

Owners Couple with two children, ages 7 and 9 years

Aspect Southwest-facing

View The back yard overlooks a coastal view

Wants and needs

- Dining area for grownups and children
- Somewhere to sit and enjoy the view
- Natural pond to attract wildlife
- Shed for bicycles and gardening tools
- Greenhouse for propagation and early vegetables
- Shelter for plants from salt-laden winds
- Space to park the owners' two cars

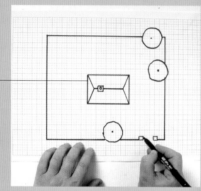

Plotting the position of the house was very important in this garden because a driveway had to be designed and budgeted for

Accurate scale plan *Where the house is in the center of the site, it is important to measure the yard accurately so that the final design fits into the available space.*

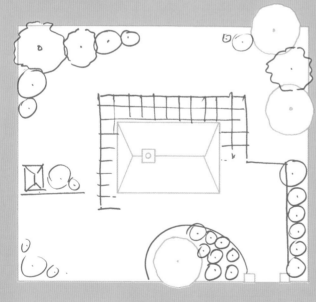

First thoughts

My initial idea was to wrap a patio around the house, to follow the sun all day. The drive was more problematic. I considered using an island bed to break up the paving, and planting a hedge along the right-hand side.

Linking front and back gardens

This second sketch shows the design becoming more fluid. The driveway is less formal and I have included a space to turn the cars. I am working with the idea of encircling the house with a lawn, linking front and back.

124

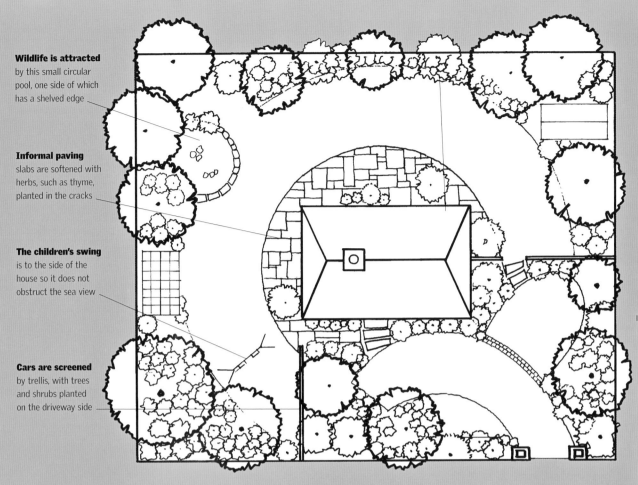

Wildlife is attracted
by this small circular pool, one side of which has a shelved edge

Informal paving
slabs are softened with herbs, such as thyme, planted in the cracks

The children's swing
is to the side of the house so it does not obstruct the sea view

Cars are screened
by trellis, with trees and shrubs planted on the driveway side

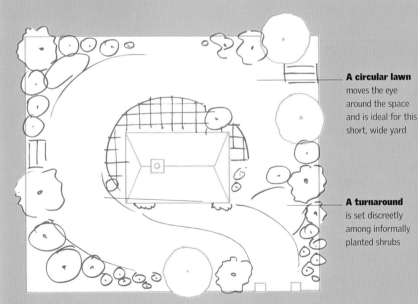

A circular lawn
moves the eye around the space and is ideal for this short, wide yard

A turnaround
is set discreetly among informally planted shrubs

Introducing a sweeping lawn

The garden is now really beginning to take shape. I still have a complete flow-through from front to back. The curved patio around the house and the sweeping lawn lead the eye through the whole space, which I feel works.

Final design

The third sketch holds the secret to this garden, but still needs some work. I have divided the garden from the drive with a screen and plantings, so that cars are not visible from the lawn when you walk around the house. The final plan has coherence: the yard is united by the lawn, which looks like a giant doughnut with the house in the central opening. A patio goes almost all the way around the house, allowing the family to follow the sun throughout the day. The front of the property is well planted; the approach to the house is fluid and very pretty. Trees and a gate set into a screen take you from the drive through to the back garden.

Designs for a sloping L-shaped garden

The drama in this garden comes from the slope; the difficulty is the corridor effect created by the alley down the side of the house. This part of the garden is also overlooked by neighboring upstairs windows. The slope was grassed over and uneven, with no level space for a dining area: terraces were needed to create more usable spaces. The owners were looking for a formal design with herbaceous borders, and they also wanted to retain a few of the mature trees.

Garden format

Garden L-shaped 80 ft x 35 ft (25 m x 11 m)

Owners Couple that loves plants and gardening

Aspect Southeast-facing

View Leafy gardens to the sides and back

Wants and needs

- Dining area close to the house
- Herbaceous plants with some structural trees
- Semi-formal design
- Somewhere to sit and view the plants
- Potager or vegetable plot
- Greenhouse to grow seeds and tender species
- Lush lawn as a foil for the plants

Scale plan *The site plan for this awkwardly shaped garden includes a cross-section of the slope, which needs to be terraced.*

Planting ideas for the arbor include a vine, honeysuckle, and hops

A wooden arbor, when planted up, will offer some shade and privacy from the neighbors

The cross-section shows the uneven surface of the slope

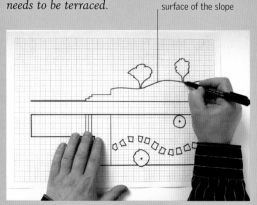

First thoughts

The yard needed terraces, but the question was how to incorporate these. I played around with informal and formal shapes, and initially thought about including a V-shaped terrace. I also gave the patio a formal touch with orderly pots.

The steps in my first sketches made the final plan almost unchanged

Clipped boxwood in pots, arranged in a symmetrical pattern, gives the patio area a formal look

The greenhouse was originally near the house, since this area is sunny, but it doesn't sit comfortably here

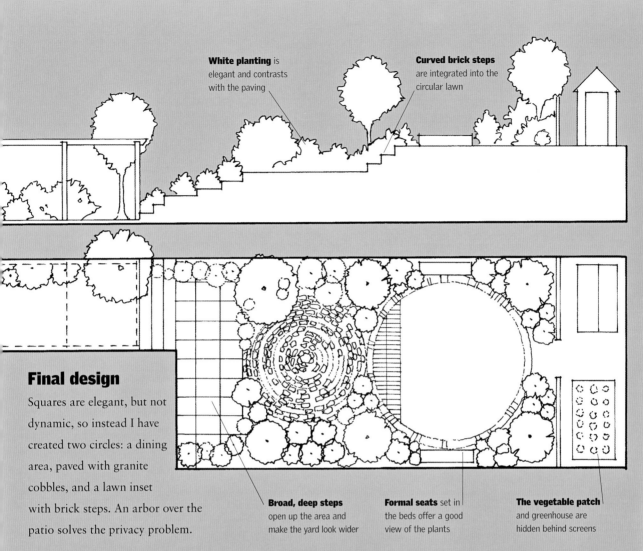

White planting is elegant and contrasts with the paving

Curved brick steps are integrated into the circular lawn

Final design

Squares are elegant, but not dynamic, so instead I have created two circles: a dining area, paved with granite cobbles, and a lawn inset with brick steps. An arbor over the patio solves the privacy problem.

Broad, deep steps open up the area and make the yard look wider

Formal seats set in the beds offer a good view of the plants

The vegetable patch and greenhouse are hidden behind screens

Formal squares

My second design focuses on two square lawns, which lend an air of formality to each of the terraces. I toyed with the idea of taller plants along the boundary next to the house to create some privacy.

Pencil-thin cypress trees are designed to create focal points

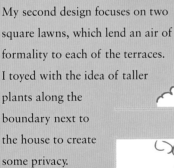

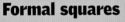

Groups of tall plants protect the patio from neighboring windows, but look unbalanced

The three terraces could be divided by reclaimed-brick walls to harmonize with the herbaceous borders

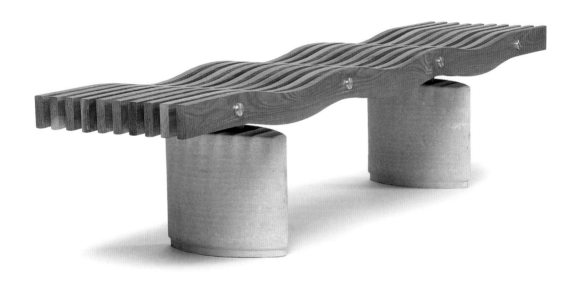

8

Choosing materials

Until fairly recently, the choice of materials for hard landscaping features in your garden wasn't great. You used what was available. That was generally local stone for patios and paths, or local wood for summerhouses. The advantage of using materials from your environment was that they had **an inherent link** with the surrounding landscape and with the building to which the garden was attached, which would also generally be constructed from local brick or stone. But now we have a much greater choice.

The range of materials available to us has broadened for a number of reasons. First, falling transportation costs have made it **viable to import materials**, even heavy stone, from all around the world. One example is the recent influx of inexpensive Chinese and Indian stone. Second, **we have become material-mad**, and are demanding more choice. This greed for choice is reflected in our home decoration and is beginning to become apparent in our gardens, too. Third, many new weather-resistant materials are available, and we have learned how to use them from books, magazines, and television programs.

When selecting materials for your outdoor space, remember, one of the most important rules is "less is more." Choose **one or two hard landscaping materials**, and make sure they suit the style of your garden, rather than simply following the latest trends. Young designers are using lots of contemporary metals, such as stainless steel and aluminum, which are fantastic for really cool, sleek gardens, but may look out of place in more traditional settings. Having said that, there's a substantial range of **very interesting new materials**, and it may also be worth revisiting some that have been out of favor for a while, such as terrazzo. This chapter explores the potential of both contemporary and traditional materials, as well as lighting and water, and shows you how to make the most of them in your designs.

Choose one or two hard landscaping materials, and make sure they suit the style of your garden, rather than simply following the latest trends

Hard landscaping for floors

As with flooring in the home, hard landscaping should reflect your garden style, and the materials should also complement the exterior walls and other architectural features. Think about its durability, and consider practicalities: how many people are going to use the space, and for what? There's no point installing metal mesh if you or your friends wear stilettos that will get caught in the gaps!

1 Industrial designs

Reinforced metal mesh used for warehouse floors and fire escapes has been employed by designer Stephen Woodhams to create these steps in his garden. Strong and versatile, the mesh has a cool, contemporary look, and is suitable for some suspended floors and roof terraces. When lit from below, the mesh's open structure throws up intriguing shadows.

2 Cast in stone

Natural stone paving may be pricy, but it is beautiful, hard-wearing— it can last a lifetime—and suits both contemporary and traditional settings. Here, Portland stone has been cut and polished for the elegant entrance to Tom Stuart-Smith's gold medal-winning 1998 RHS Chelsea Flower Show garden.

Sandstone is another type of natural stone used extensively in garden landscaping. It is available in different finishes and colors, and, like many stone products, it can be cut to size or bought as standard-sized pavers.

Indian and Chinese imports have brought down the cost of many types of natural stone, and some is now no more expensive than manufactured imitations. However, the quality of imported stone is not always great: it can be very porous, and may need to be chemically sealed to prevent it from staining.

3 Mediterranean moods
Originally used in warmer climates, paving, such as terracotta tiles, has become increasingly popular in cooler countries. Terracotta looks and feels warm, and makes a great foil for planting, but be careful, since not all products are frostproof. Check with your supplier that their tiles will survive the winter in your garden.

4 Mix and match
Mixing flooring materials can be very effective, but it is easy to get carried away. A rule of thumb is to use very few different materials, and to keep your design simple. The garden here uses slate tiles broken up by light-toned Yorkstone pavers, which mirror the color of the brick raised beds behind. Slate is hard-wearing, but because it is slippery when wet and dark in color, avoid laying it in damp, shady areas.

5 Color and texture
When combining materials, use complementary or contrasting colors and textures. Here, pale gray Yorkstone pavers contrast with blue-black engineering bricks to form the upper level, and also add an interesting textural contrast to the cobbles on the lower level.

6 Contemporary strength
Designer Roger Bradley used aluminum flooring for his garden at the 2002 RHS Chelsea Flower Show. It has an urban look, and is commonly used for suspended walkways in industrial buildings. Strong, durable and lightweight, it works well in roof gardens and on balconies, but remember that it can get hot when exposed to sun and become uncomfortable to walk on barefoot. You can buy it from specialists in industrial flooring.

8

CHOOSING MATERIALS **HARD LANDSCAPING FOR FLOORS**

133

Natural, textured flooring

Natural materials blend beautifully with planting. Wood, riven stone, gravel, and grass all have great textures and can work well with smooth, manufactured materials, such as steel. Use your natural flooring in broad expanses, where its beauty can be best appreciated, and choose hard-wearing products, such as stone, for frequently used areas.

1 Stone "planks"

Despite their appearance, the "planks" in this garden are dressed stone, not wood, and have been laid as decking around rocks at the water's edge. Spaces between the lengths are filled with loose stones that add texture and interest to this hard-wearing floor.

2 Verticals and horizontals

Simplicity is the key to Diana Yakeley's design. The natural timber decking, which features a galvanized steel rill filled with glass cubes, butts up to a slatted bench, creating an interesting contrast of vertical and horizontal lines. This idea is carried through with the vertical stems of the black bamboo (*Phyllostachys nigra*) planted behind the bench. Hard- or softwood can be used for decking. Hardwood lasts longer but is more expensive, and you need to check that it is from an environmentally sustainable source before you buy.

3 Versatile gravel

Wispy tufts of the ornamental grass *Festuca glauca* are used here in conjunction with sweeping arcs of gravel and cobbles. Gravel, when laid over a weed-suppressing membrane, keeps maintenance to a minimum and makes a good foil for grasses and Mediterranean plants. It is available in different grades, from fine shingle to larger chips, and in a range of natural and bright colors.

4 In tune with nature

Designed by Mark Walker and Sarah Wigglesworth for the 2002 RHS Chelsea Flower Show, the theme of this unusual garden is sustainability. The wooden walkway runs through reed beds, which are natural water cleansers, and is decorated with blue steel steps and fencing to create a simple yet striking design.

5 Harmonizing textures

In Joe Swift's design, a range of natural materials create this textured floor. Rugged slate chips are laid between leaf-shaped beds of fine turf. The beds are edged with strips of aluminum to form a dramatic contrast. This is a versatile metal, but it has sharp edges and should not be used as a veneer in gardens for children.

6 Shallow steps

Alexandra Bonnin's design, "*La Main Coulante*" or "Flowing Banisters," for the Chaumont International Garden Festival, features a series of shallow terraces that step down between parasol pines. Each terrace is alternately laid with terracotta- and ocher-colored gravel, and the risers are edged with ribbons of steel. This bold, simple design would work equally well in a smaller garden.

7 Hard and soft

These large, rocky stepping stones surrounded by mossy grass form a beautiful natural path in Patrick Watson's design. The hard stone and the soft grass create a great combination of color and texture.

Walls and screens

Not so long ago, trellis and hedging were the only options for walls and screens, but now all kinds of weatherproof materials are available. Take samples into your garden to be sure the textures and colors blend with your style. And remember that too many hard surfaces can look uninviting, so always use planting or some color to soften the overall effect.

1 Curved concrete
Used with imagination, concrete is a beautiful material. It can be molded into almost any shape and contrasts brilliantly with lush planting. This amazing concrete pavilion in the Piccadilly Gardens, Manchester, England, was designed by Japanese architect Tadao Ando. The curved structure screens the gardens from the noisy streets; a scaled-down version would offer similar protection in a small yard.

2 Copper and glass
Glass brick walls are good devices for directing the eye around a garden without blocking out light. I used them for this tunnel, which frames a decorative screen beyond. The screen is made from copper, which takes on a wonderful verdigris patina as it weathers.

3 Mexican influence
American landscape architect Martha Schwartz is famed for her vibrant designs. The painted Mexican-style concrete-walled rooms in this private garden in Texas offer shade and a graphic shadow play throughout the day.

4 Textured effect
This simple low retaining wall, built from textured granite blocks, mirrors the grasses and tree bark, demonstrating a perfect harmony between hard and soft landscaping.

5 Nature's way

Made from twisted branches, this fence blends beautifully with the surrounding landscape. It also has a practical function, protecting walkers along a coastal path.

6 Abbey inspiration

The remains of a 12th-century abbey are integrated into the gardens at Tresco, Isles of Scilly. I have used clay brick in one of my own designs to create a similar effect. Rock plants and ferns, squeezed into the cracks between the stones, soften the hard surfaces and bring the wall to life.

7 Mesh screens

I am a big fan of wire mesh and use it a lot in my designs. It acts a bit like a sheer curtain, allowing light in but still creating a sense of enclosure. The mesh here is rippled to give it an ephemeral quality.

8 Leaves of steel

Leaflike shapes cut into brushed stainless steel form this dynamic screen in a garden by designers Philippe Herlin and Daniel Jud. Unfortunately, it fights with the beautiful herbaceous plants in front, and would be more effective against a bolder planting plan.

9 Bamboo tunnel

Naturally versatile and strong, bamboo has many uses in the garden. Here, large canes set in rows create a frame that guides the eye through to a large pot of living bamboo.

10 Acrylic perspectives

David Finch's garden at the 2003 Westonbirt Festival used sliding screens made from acrylic laminated with radiant films. The screens reflected different colors, and "projected" them onto the gravel and plantings behind.

Furniture and sculpture

Choosing furniture and sculpture is a personal decision: no one, not even a garden designer, can make it for you. Furniture should be comfortable, but also functional and decorative. Choosing sculpture is more difficult. Try to borrow a piece from the sculptor, and live with it before making a decision to buy. Be bold, and remember that little pieces often make little impact.

1

USING SCULPTURE

When choosing sculpture for your garden, the first rule is to find a piece that complements your garden style. A classical stone statue makes a great statement when used to punctuate the end of a path in a formal garden, while an abstract piece can enhance a contemporary or Modernist style.

The material you select should also suit your space, unless you are making a conscious decision to create conflict. Natural materials blend into most settings, but modern metals and plastics look out of place in naturalistic or cottage-style designs.

One large dramatic sculpture, used as a focal point, is generally better than a few smaller pieces scattered throughout the yard that fight each other for attention.

1 Floating spheres
Bold and bright, these balloons set the tone for the futuristic designs at the Chaumont Festival, France.

2 Abstract torso
This sculpture of a torso is by John Skelton and stands in the Gibberd Garden in Essex, England.

3 All meshed up
"*Mente la Menta*", designed by Charles Hawes for the Chaumont Festival, is made from steel mesh.

5 Spiked beauty
These rods topped with glass stars were designed by Neil Wilkinson for the Westonbirt Garden Festival.

2

3

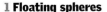

5

7

8

SELECTING FURNITURE

We give great thought to the style and type of furniture for our homes, but in the garden not so much care is taken.

Furniture can make or break a garden, adding to your comfort and the enjoyment you get from your yard. Think carefully during the design stage about what you want and how the furniture will be used. This avoids the problem of a patio that's too small for the dining table and chairs you've chosen, or a hammock you dreamed about but have no place to hang in the finished Eden. Go shopping, measure up chairs, benches, and tables, and remember that most furniture needs a hard, stable surface to sit on. As with sculpture, select furniture that complements the garden style.

4 Timeless teak

Designed by Charlotte Sanderson, this roof garden features a teak table and chairs, complemented by limestone paving, decking, and an Italian polished plaster wall.

6 Fine lines

Brilliantly versatile, intricate ironwork furniture adds a French flavor to a garden design.

7 Lazy days

Hammocks offer a great way to relax, and suit informal settings.

8 Swing low

This blue swing seat, designed by Paula Rainey Crofts, harmonizes well with soft, romantic planting.

9 Rustic charms

Woven from vines, this bench looks good but may be uncomfortable.

10 Compact dining

Designed by Declan Buckley, this small London garden features a compact table and matching stools.

Structures and buildings

A garden room allows you to work, rest, and enjoy your outdoor space from a different perspective. It also lengthens the time you spend in the garden, enticing you outside in any weather to experience the changing seasons. Make sure your room, gazebo, or pavilion either matches the overall feel of the garden or contrasts with it to create an exciting architectural focal point.

1

1 Glass effects

Building a conservatory onto your home not only creates a light and airy living space, but, seen from a garden perspective, offers visual excitement. Sleek, contemporary glass buildings create an exciting contrast when attached to historic town houses, such as this one in London. They look especially magical at night, when foliage and flowers are caught in the glow of their lights.

2 Points of interest

Most garden structures are about providing shelter or storage. But sometimes they're built purely for fun, or to make a design statement. This wire mesh room, for example, was designed by Factory Furniture for one of my garden designs. It provides a quirky but beautiful focal point over a shallow pool, as well as a place for contemplation.

3 Decorative folly

Follies are great fun. The 19th-century rococo folly at Elton Hall in Shropshire is a fine example of this eccentric form of garden architecture. It looks like a tiny Indian palace, and makes a highly decorative focal point at the end of the lawn, as well as providing a sheltered place to sit.

4

5

4 Vantage point

The wooden pavilion, by Mirabel Osler, is reminiscent of colorful Caribbean architecture. It has a gently curving roof supported by decorative panels. Inside, the comfortable wooden box seats, scattered with cushions, offer a lovely place from which to admire the garden.

5 Balanced structures

The gardens at Hestercombe, England, were originally designed in the early 20th century by landscape architect Sir Edwin Lutyens and Gertrude Jekyll, whose planting plans are now legendary. The pair worked together on many projects, but Hestercombe is considered to be their most accomplished creation. This image shows the stone alcove and steps leading to the sunken garden, and is just one example of the symmetry, balance, and proportion of the structures in these beautiful gardens.

6 Living roofscape

In many Scandinavian countries, turf is used to insulate the roofs of cabins or wooden buildings, such as this one in Finland. Grass is very effective, keeping properties warm throughout the freezing winter months. Recently, there has been a proposal by environmental groups to "green up" the roofs of buildings in London. The idea is that turf not only insulates, but would also help to reduce harmful carbon dioxide levels in the city—plants absorb this gas, and release oxygen into the atmosphere.

Water features

Dynamic, versatile, and beautiful, water can perform many roles, regardless of your yard size. Remember to make it safe first. In gardens for children, fix a sturdy grille over the top of your pond to prevent them from falling in, and avoid slippery surfaces close to water to safeguard people of all ages. Use water to create exciting effects, from still, reflecting pools to sculptural waterfalls.

1 The vortex
This circular pool forms the focal point of Andy Sturgeon's design for the RHS Chelsea Flower Show. Water spills into it from an upper level, while a metal fluted sculpture sucks water down into a vortex. The splashing and movement fires the design with energy.

2 Calming pools
John Thompson's "The Diamond Light" garden, shown at the 2003 Westonbirt Garden Festival, features beautiful glass sculptures set in a tranquil pool. The sculptures, made from slices of tinted glass, resemble rocks, and hint at the Japanese designs that influenced Thompson. The reflections from the glass and water evoke a calm, peaceful atmosphere in the garden.

3 Cube of color
The size of your yard shouldn't deter you from using water in your design. Here, a small metal cube inset with a bright red bowl and a small fountain makes an intriguing focal point in this contemporary setting.

4 Mexican mood
This patio pool is beautiful and elegant. The traditional Mexican white stucco grotto, with its turquoise water, lush vines, ferns, and bamboos, provides a cooling retreat where the owners can relax during the heat of the day.

4

5 Natural effects

Natural-looking ponds and pools, such as this one, offer many benefits. Still water reflects the changing patterns in the sky, and attracts insects and wildlife. A new pond will be filled with frogs and toads within a year or two, and birds will visit every day to drink and bathe. Make sure that one side of your pond slopes gently to allow small mammals, reptiles, and amphibians to get in and out easily.

6 Stream of steps

This dramatic cascade of water and steps set on a hillside in the gardens at Terrasson, France, reflects landscape artist Kathryn Gustafson's great skill. It enhances the natural landscape, powering down the hill with vital momentum.

7 Falling water

Waterfalls are energizing, exciting features for large gardens. This magnificent structure has been designed to imitate nature, but, unless you happen to be a member of the Osbourne family and your garden is in Hollywood, it's not a practical idea for a suburban yard. To be effective, it should blend into the surrounding landscape.

8 Light reflections

The owners of this home in Wiltshire, England, have built a pond directly outside their window, where it throws light into the house, and allows them to view the aquatic plants and wildlife close up, whatever the weather.

7

8

Lighting your garden

The role of garden lights is twofold: they help to guide you around your yard or up steps at night, and they add a little bit of magic to your designs. Plan your lighting design carefully, and don't be tempted to use too many different effects or styles. Look for new types of lighting, such as fiber optics and adapted neon, which are becoming more widely available for domestic garden use.

1 Palm lights

Floodlighting—where lights are set up high and the beams directed down onto the ground—tends to be used to light a large area, such as a football stadium, but it can also create some fun effects. The colorful neon lights fixed beneath the spiky fronds of these tall palms have a surreal, retro club look.

2 The sun and the moon

The water feature in Stephen Woodhams' "Sanctuary" garden uses light to great effect. During the day, the circular glass disk in the metal screen reflects light to resemble the sun; at night it is backlit to echo the moon.

3 Nightlife in the city

You will find lots of inspiration for garden lighting in a city. Look at the ways in which buildings are illuminated, and take these ideas home with you. The lighting on this roof terrace in London is quite subtle, allowing the owners to enjoy the garden at night without washing out the theatrical effect of the cityscape in the distance.

4 Tree lights

Lights strung from trees confer a contemporary look. Lace tiny white lights through the branches to mimic stars, or hang up lamps to create an intimate "room" beneath the canopy. The opaque shades used here soften the light and would be ideal above a seating or dining area.

5 Safe steps

Lighting can be purely decorative, or serve a function, but the best designs combine both. Garden steps should always be illuminated to prevent accidents—in this design, every other tread of the sweeping staircase is lit by a single spotlight recessed into the walls. The lighting is a safety feature, but it is also an integral part of the elegant design. To achieve the same harmony, make sure the lighting in your garden complements the style.

6 Contemporary uplights

The lighting on these containers is simple but effective. Spotlights set into the deck highlight one side of the pots, casting dramatic shadows.

LIGHTING EFFECTS

Garden designers have borrowed exciting lighting effects from theater designers. Here are a few ideas to consider:

Spotlighting

Pick out a plant or special feature by training a spotlight on it.

Grazing

Position a light to graze the facade of a building, feature, or plant to highlight its texture or details.

Floodlighting

Fix lights up high on a building or in a tree and focus the beam down.

Uplighting

Place lights below a plant, tree, or feature to illuminate their leaves, branches and textures.

Backlighting

Light your feature from behind to throw it into silhouette.

Mirroring

Illuminate the front of a feature or plant close to water to create a mirrored image in the surface.

Underwater lighting

Most effective where the water is clear, and the lights illuminate a feature, such as a fountain.

5

6

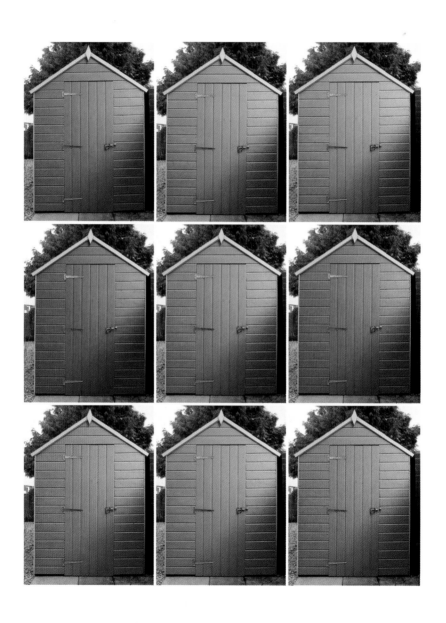

9

Using color

All gardens are full of color, mainly various shades of green. The natural world offers us **a rainbow of possibilities**: flowers lure insects and brighten our lives with their colorful petals, while leaves provide backdrops of green, burgundy, yellow, silver, or glaucous blue.

Of course, color isn't just about plants. Materials and paint are used extensively in gardens, too, adding to the kaleidoscopic effect. In countries that have the benefit of brilliant sunlight, walls are often painted vibrant shades of pink, blue, and yellow. Renowned Mexican architect **Luis Barragán**, for example, created a famous stable yard in the 1960s at San Cristobal, where, instead of the usual stark Modernist white, he **painted walls pink**. Such daring use of color revolutionized people's ideas, and Barragán's style continues to influence contemporary garden designers, such as Martha Schwartz (*right*). In the past ten years, there has been a rush in cooler countries to use bold colors possibly more suited to areas with strong light, but **the trend is now moving toward a more neutral palette**.

The psychology of color—how it affects us emotionally—has long interested artists and gardeners alike. Gertrude Jekyll, working in the early 20th century, appreciated the power of color, and used her artistic eye to **create evocative images** by carefully combining flowering plants of different shades. But you don't have to be an artist to know that red is a stimulating color—its link with danger is no coincidence—while soft pastel blues are calming. The skill is to translate this innate knowledge into a design, manipulating colors to produce different looks. You can combine muted shades for subtle contrasts in naturalistic gardens, or mix vivid colors in a modern setting to startle and surprise. In this chapter, I hope to demonstrate **the effects you can achieve** with colorful plants and hard landscaping, and to show how these can be integrated into your final design solutions.

Combine muted shades for subtle contrasts in naturalistic gardens, or mix vivid colors in a modern setting to startle and surprise

Infinite shades of green

I come from Ireland, a country famed for its 40 shades of green. In reality, though, it has hundreds, and this multitude of tones isn't limited to my homeland. Green is the color of vegetation the world over, and in the garden it provides the base that allows all other colors to shine.

Our world is awash with green: delicate, pink-tinged spring buds; firm, promising shoots; sturdy stems; unfurling and mature leaves; and lush carpets of lawn. Green also affects our mood and has healing qualities: it is soothing and helps us to relax, both mentally and physically. In color therapy, green is considered beneficial for mild depression, anxiety, and nervousness. No wonder we feel uplifted when we go for a walk in the country or stroll through our gardens, and architects and city planners include green spaces to break up monotonous urban gray.

Creating impact So ubiquitous is the color green that it's easy to take it for granted and forget its impact in terms of design. Like a pretty but old wallpaper, we know it's there but we rarely give it a second thought. Yet it is *the* most important color in the garden.

A garden full of colorful flowers has far greater impact against a green tapestry, while some formal and contemporary designs rely almost entirely on greens of different shades—including emerald, sage, and lime—to color in the spaces between the hard landscaping.

Experiment with green foliage plants in your garden, and see what moods and effects you can create. Dark foliage provides depth and acts as a foil for light or bright colors, such as yellow, scarlet, and white. Choose brilliant yellow-greens for their energizing and zesty qualities, or try velvety sage greens with warm tones to contrast with pale yellows, pinks, and mauves.

1 *Santolina chamaecyparissus* var. *nana*
2 *Ophiopogon planiscapus* 'Nigrescens' and *Stachys byzantina*
3 Agave species
4 *Hosta sieboldiana*
5 *Stipa tenuissima*
6 *Ballota* 'All Hallows Green'
7 *Geranium* 'Blue Sunrise'
8 *Cornus alba* 'Aurea'
9 *Dryopteris wallichiana*
10 *Parthenocissus henryana*
11 *Arum italicum* subsp. *italicum* 'Marmoratum'
12 *Pulmonaria* 'Ocupol'
13 *Melianthus major*
14 *Acer palmatum*
15 *Asarum europaeum*
16 *Pinus mugo* 'Mops'.

Static color

Garden designers employ two types of color: transient plant color that changes throughout the seasons, and static color, which is essentially unchanging color, such as that provided by mosaic containers and painted trellis.

There has been a trend among contemporary designers to use vivid static colors to surprise or provide an eye-catching focal point. This color, painted on walls or features, adds impact to the architecture, and can be contrasted with more subtle, transient plant colors. Bright hues are best used in hot countries that are bathed in strong light, such as those in the Mediterranean, Africa, and Asia. But give careful consideration to your choice of color where the light is weaker, since some shades, such as the insipid blues that were popular in the UK and Ireland for a while, look muddy and dull under cloudy skies.

Color, of course, is a very personal thing. Start by selecting colors you like, and try out different swatches. Paint small sections of wall or fence and place your proposed plants or features in front before committing to a larger area.

1 Mirror image
Cleverly positioned by the edge of a pool, this pink, fish-shaped, sculptural screen is mirrored in the water. This creates a great 3-D effect, and also paints a picture where one block of color remains static while the other shimmers and moves.

2 Under the sun
Strong colors, such as this orange and striking cobalt blue, come to life in the sun. The scene looks like a stage set, complete with special effects lighting that casts dramatic shadows and brings out different tones and colors.

3 Awash with color
Blocks of lime green and white perfectly complement the sparkling turquoise water spilling out into the pool below. Together, the water and graphic colors create a harmonious and calming whole.

4 Dancing shadows

Painted walls can be used like movie screens. If you place plants or artifacts, such as these urns, in front, the light projects cinematic shadows that glide and dance as the sun moves across the sky.

5 Hot and fiery

This bright red wall looks dazzling in the intense sun of its Las Vegas desert location. Steve Martino, the designer, has positioned it close to a tree so the shadows cast by the branches add texture to the smooth surface. The taupe soft furnishings in front of it offer a soothing contrast.

6 Vibrant spots

A curved wall is dotted with transparent colored disks in this dynamic design. Large neutral expanses punctuated with hints of contrasting color can create more impact than a single bright shade used in a block. As light passes through these disks, the wall glows with luminous colors.

7 Textured blue

The quirky blue wooden tiles in this garden lead the eye through the space, adding interest to what would otherwise have been an unremarkable pathway. Setting the decking squares at alternate angles also introduces pattern and texture to the design.

8 Surreal trees

Acrylic is increasingly used in contemporary gardens, and is available in a wide range of colors. Here, pink and blue screens mask white-barked birches, giving them a surreal, iridescent quality.

Transient color

Color in the plant world is constantly changing: spring bulbs in vibrant yellows, pinks, and blues are replaced by summer flowers of every hue, followed in fall by a blaze of fiery shades as the leaves change color before they drop. Even evergreens start out in spring with pale or colorful young shoots, which darken as they mature.

The skill of the designer is to combine these colors to create an everlasting display, or a crescendo of seasonal color. Gertrude Jekyll, an artist who became one of the 20th century's foremost plantswomen, experimented with a stunning palette of colors. She used flowering plants, graduating their colors from cool to warm shades, and then back to cool through the length of the border. Fascinated by the effect that color could achieve, her philosophy was to lead the eye gently from one tone to another. But Jekyll had the luxury of space—she designed sections of the garden that could be hidden from view in the winter when the flowers were over.

Contemporary gardeners with smaller yards have to be more aware of seasonal changes that leave gaps in planting—and color—plans. Consider carefully how your chosen plants will perform at different times of the year: include specimens to entertain early in spring, planted between later performers that will continue the show as the seasons progress. Make sure your plants' colors complement or contrast with their immediate neighbors, and the whole collection.

Autumn glory *Trees and shrubs that offer fall color are a must for all gardens, large and small. The dazzling display in this wood shows the effects that can be achieved.*

Color through the year
The pictures here show clearly how the color in this beautiful garden at Park Farm, Essex, England, changes as the seasons turn.

1 & 2 Spring
The season is heralded with the beautiful deep maroon flowers of *Tulipa* 'Mariette', which are then succeeded by the brilliant white blooms of *Lunaria annua*.

3 Early summer
As spring turns into summer, lollipop-like alliums parade above blue aquilegia. Dainty forget-me-nots line the path, while a column-shaped conifer, *Juniperus communis* 'Hibernica', adds a vertical accent to the back of the bed.

4 & 5 Summer
The repeat-flowering, powerfully scented *Rosa* 'Louise Odier' lines the pathway at the beginning of summer with spots of rich pink. Later in the season, the garden is awash with rich greens and pretty white daisies.

6 Autumn
The herbaceous borders are shutting down for the winter, but before they disappear, they decorate the garden with subtle browns and oranges, while the lawn and remaining leaves provide an enduring green.

7 Winter
Dried twigs and stems are dusted with frost in winter, covering beds and borders with a white veil.

Combining static and transient color

Color in a garden is rarely derived from either just static or just transient color, and combining both will help you achieve many more wonderful effects. Look for areas of the garden where you can introduce color in either form, matching similar shades or using bold contrasts for visual impact.

Many people forget that their boundaries and fences can provide useful static color to offset planting. Take a closer look at yours, and ensure that any unfinished wooden fences that have bleached to a dirty gray are not neutralizing the beautiful colors of the planting in front. Even gray concrete walls, a common background in Europe, can be painted to provide smooth, colorful backdrops. I regard lawns as static color, too—they offer a soothing green carpet against which darker greens or brightly colored flowering shrubs and plants may be displayed. In fact, because our gardens are predominantly green, this is a good color to experiment with as a background for brighter shades.

In hot countries, vivid blues, magenta, and yellows look startling with foliage and flowers in front. But in cooler, northern climates, deeper colors, such as dark eggplant, navy blue, and black, look wonderful with foliage pressed up against them, especially if your design is energetic and startling rather than restful. To achieve a more peaceful scene, use the colors of local stone against herbaceous planting. Or contrast neutral shades with splashes of bright color to provide vibrant accents. Tacky can be fun!

1 Cool blues

Although white isn't officially a color, it works well as a clean canvas, bringing out the pigments of the colors in front. Blue is normally recessive and easily lost among other shades, but when combined with white, it is enriched and given prominence.

2 Seeing red

It's rare to see so much red in a garden, since most people shy away from rich colors. The design of this roof terrace is successful because the color palette is very limited. A dark red wall highlights the white-stemmed birches and pale limestone floor, and the red chair links inside with out.

3 Homage to Mondrian

A tribute to Dutch abstract artist Piet Mondrian, this flouts the design rules concerning color in the garden by combining bright primary colors in both soft- and hard-landscaping materials. A brave idea that is effective here.

4 Tulips forever

Give your lawn a lift at any time of the year with colorful wooden or ceramic flowers. These hot-pink tulips are great fun, and provide a dramatic contrast with the cool green grass and blue conservatory.

5 Muted metal

Paints and plants aren't the only materials that inject color into the garden. Metals offer subtle shades, but it is their reflective quality that makes them so useful. Corrugated iron is an exciting choice: light bounces off the ripples, creating wonderful colors and patterns. Its silvery tones also complement the yellow and blue-green grasses in this design.

6 Flaming effects

The designers of this show garden used a combination of flame-colored cannas and copper to evoke a fiery volcano theme. The strong reds and pinks also draw out the red undertones in the blue-purple back wall, while cool, lush greens temper the hot hues.

7 Picked out in purple

These beds of purple agapanthus flanking a simple rectangular lawn are stunning in themselves, but they're really set off by the two purple loungers on the patio. Transient colors are normally supplied by plants, but here both the planting and accessories are temporary. It may be excessive to purchase a selection of chairs to match your seasonal planting, but you can use pots painted in coordinating shades to achieve a similar effect.

8 Blue on blue

Combining shades of the same color can be extremely effective, as this simple blue container filled with lavender proves.

Add color to your plan

If you're feeling a bit nervous about adding color to your garden, try photocopying your plans and shading in areas with colored pencils. This will give you a rough idea of where you want colored plants, flowers, and features in your design, and how well they work together. Also paste images torn from magazines onto a large sheet of paper to create a mood board to inspire you.

White dominates the planting in the first part of the garden. White is both elegant and bright, reflecting light onto the cobbled circular patio

Contemporary green

The young couple who own this urban garden wanted something contemporary. The result is a yard filled with luxurious green foliage plants. The blossom of two existing trees—a cherry and laburnum—provide bursts of pink spring and yellow summer color, which are all the more dramatic against the sea of green around them.

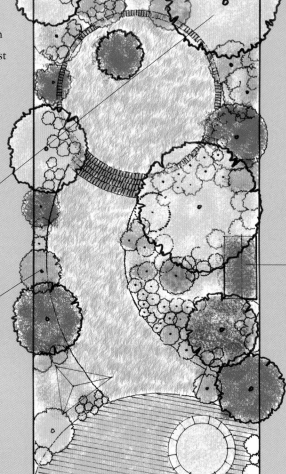

The yellow, pealike flowers of this laburnum drip from the stems in late spring and early summer

Echoing the greens of the plants surrounding it, the garden shed is almost camouflaged by the foliage next to the boundary fence

Architectural green foliage plants characterize this garden, combining a range of exciting shapes and textures to provide year-round interest

Refreshing citrus tones, including zesty yellow and orange daylilies, fill the beds surrounding the raised, circular lawn

A luxurious green lawn provides a cool foil for the hot-hued planting plan wrapped around it

Whites and brights

A combination of color palettes has been used in this design. A white garden—inspired by Vita Sackville-West's design at Sissinghurst, England—starts things off, but gives way to zesty colors, such as yellow and orange, at the end of the yard.

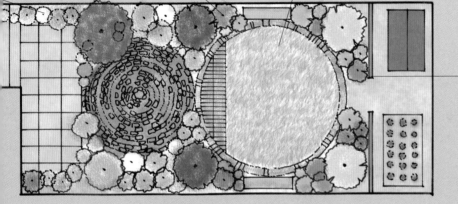

Terracotta-colored walls or trellis hide the greenhouse and vegetable plot and complement the colorful planting

Seaside lavenders, blues and yellows

For this garden with sea views, I decided to use purples and blues in various tones, highlighted with complementary shades of yellow—mostly in the form of structural euphorbias and aromatic santolinas. Plants were chosen both for their color and for their ability to withstand salt-laden sea breezes.

Planted between sandstone paving slabs, groups of lavender and low-growing thyme inject spots of color

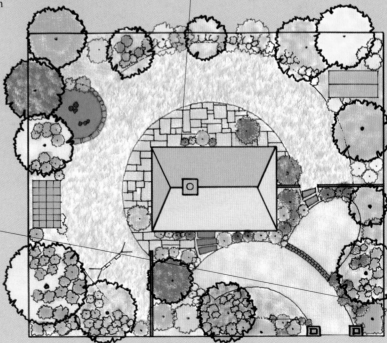

Blue and yellow are complementary colors, and the yellow-green, torchlike stems of this euphorbia look great against the pretty blue flowers of bugle

159

10
Designing with plants

The premise of this book is to offer a basic guide to designing your garden, and to explain the ground rules in an order that's easy to follow. But planting is a rather more complex affair, and to reduce it to one simple step in the overall design process is to do a fascinating subject an injustice. What I will offer are some guidelines; it's then up to you to **go out and explore** the world of plants. Start your research by cutting out pictures from magazines, and jotting down the names of plants that you see on television programs. Dig out gardening books, too, and ask your friends and neighbors what grows well in their gardens. Use your notebook to **build up a bank of knowledge** about plants that you'd like to use in your final plans. Take your time, and separate this job from the overall task of designing.

At the same time, look through Chapter 6 (*see p102*) of this book, which shows you how to **assess your site, soil, and local conditions**. Armed with this knowledge, select plants that will be at home in your garden.

When you have compiled a list of suitable plants, **the design work can begin**. One of the most difficult tasks is combining plant colors, textures, and forms to harmonize with the **style and essence of the garden** you have designed. You also have to factor in scent, seasonal interest, and the way the planting plan will develop and grow over time. For inspiration and guidance, I've described a few of the most popular planting styles, although these by no means represent a definitive list. Styles have evolved over many centuries, and there are many different philosophies regarding **how and where to use plants**. But the real fun comes as you develop the confidence to build up your own repertoire, and create a planting plan that reflects your individual taste. By learning about plants through observation, practical experience, and making a few mistakes, you can design your dream garden.

Planting is a complex affair, and to reduce it to one simple step in the overall design process is to do a fascinating subject an injustice

Planting styles

There are many planting styles to choose from, but here are four of the most popular. You can follow them exactly, or use them as rough guides.

Mixed planting

Combining a mixed palette of plants is one of the most practical solutions for borders in small gardens, or areas of larger gardens that can be seen from the house throughout the year. A mixed planting style provides continuous seasonal interest, and is a successful fusion of medium to large architectural trees and shrubs, offering background structure, shape and form; focal plants that catch the eye in borders or containers; and herbaceous plants, bedding, and bulbs that fill the gaps, adding color and a seasonal lift to the overall design.

Cottage planting

This traditional style can be defined as very English, very flowery, and very romantic. Gertrude Jekyll perfected what we now consider to be cottage garden planting. She used groups of hardy herbaceous perennials in loose, lozenge-shaped swaths, and contrasted textures, forms, and colors to create a naturalistic effect. This style is demanding, requiring good plant knowledge and quite a lot of maintenance. The herbaceous plants peak in the summer, but most die down in winter, leaving you with uninspiring beds of bare soil and brown stalks.

Trees and shrubs form the building blocks of the design

Focal plants that call out for attention create highlights in the border

Flowering perennials, annuals and bulbs offer seasonal interest

Plants in groups of at least five form dramatic swaths

Contrasting colors, textures, and shapes create a tapestry effect

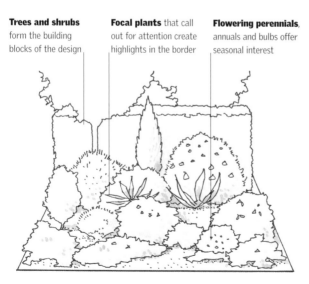

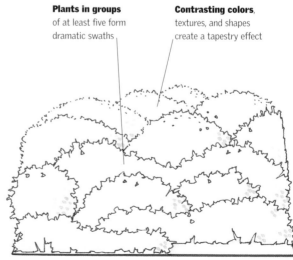

Modernist planting

By Modernist planting, I don't mean "contemporary". Modernism, a movement that took off at the beginning of the 20th century, was primarily a school of art, architecture, and furniture design, although its influence on garden design was not established until later in the century. The Modernist style still has relevance for garden designers today, and is achieved using plants in blocks, with designs based on grids, reminiscent of Mondrian paintings. The grid formations, natural planting, and structure and form are as important as flower color.

Architectural plants provide graphic, clean shapes and offer focus

Clipped hedges can be used to define the boundaries of the yard

Planting in blocks reflects Mondrian's Modernist paintings

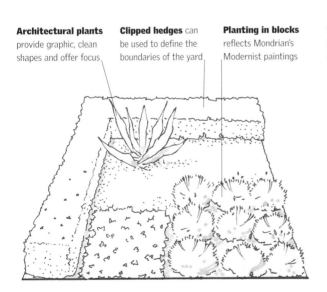

Naturalistic planting

Mirroring the way plants grow in nature, this style uses mostly native species set out in random groups or drifts. The designer takes note of the site and soil and selects either indigenous plants or imported ones that will flourish without becoming invasive. Herbaceous grasses and perennials are used extensively, but because only tough species that need no feeding or staking are selected, maintenance is relatively low, and the dried flower heads and parched grasses are often left to stand over winter. This is a beautiful style for a large informal or wildlife garden.

Structural foliage plants provide a permanent framework

Grasses add form and texture, and rustle and sway in the breeze

Repeated uprights act as focal points, emboldening the design

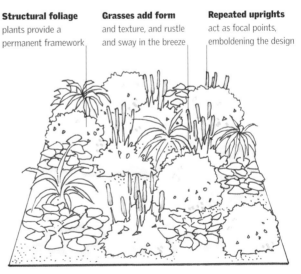

Mixed planting

To create a unified mixed planting plan that offers year-round interest, you need a balance of different types of plants. This means using both evergreen and deciduous trees and shrubs, herbaceous perennials that add occasional sparkle at different times of the year, and a selection of flowering bulbs, corms and tubers, plus any annuals or alpines that light your fire.

The trick is to orchestrate these plants to achieve a harmonious balance of color and structure. Position your structural plants first, since these form the bones of your design. And allow space for specimens that stand out from the crowd and draw the eye. Lastly, fill the gaps with seasonal flowers. Use restraint by not including too many different plants, and pack your design with excitement, using flourishes of dramatic color backed by a steady sea of green.

1

1 Neat structure

Conifers can be useful in small gardens because they offer permanent structure. Many are neat and compact, but some become giants, so check the labels carefully. Here, they are used to punctuate the start of a path, and as foils for perennials and summer annuals. Conifers tend to suck moisture from the soil, so choose bedfellows that don't mind dry conditions.

2 Colorful mix

The planting in this family garden is designed to provide year-round color and interest. Evergreen herbs, such as lavender and purple-leaved sage, are mixed with shrubs, including a low-growing ceanothus, azaleas, and a yellow-flowered hypericum. White Regal lilies act as focals.

3 Creative composition

Christopher Lloyd is a master of color and form. This garden at his home at Great Dixter is enclosed by yew hedging, and given form with structural plants, such as *Cotoneaster horizontalis* and *Acer palmatum* 'Shishigashira'. Focal plants include *Arundo donax* by the pond, pampas, and *Calamagrostis* 'Karl Foerster', together with dazzling blood-red dahlias and *Canna* 'Striata'.

4 Exotic accents

Large trees in this Australian garden act as a backdrop for the spiky cordylines, while *Melianthus major*, planted *en masse*, and blue echiums provide infill.

167

Naturalistic planting

One of the most popular forms of naturalistic planting is "prairie style," which takes its inspiration from natural habitats, such as the American prairies, and mimics the way grasses and herbaceous plants grow there. It's a relaxed style, where plants are allowed to self-seed and intermingle. A small selection of different species that are well suited to the soil, exposure, and local conditions are repeated throughout the plan. Prairie style uses no built structures—the structure is derived from the plants themselves. It also requires an artistic eye, and is most effective on a large scale. It can look messy early in the year when rain has turned the overwintering stems and grasses to mush.

Another popular style is meadow planting. Ideal for gardens large or small, a meadow can

be especially beautiful in an orchard setting, but remember that it won't look good all year. Grow a mix of grasses and wild flowers on poor soil, which prevents rampant grasses from taking over. Meadow planting uses many native plants that are disappearing from our countryside, and is in tune with the natural rhythm of the environment.

1

2

3

1 Wild ways

"Prairie planting" captures the wild landscapes of the American prairies with large groupings of grasses and herbaceous perennials, such as the yellow rudbeckias and pink echinaceas shown here. These plants are happiest on relatively poor soil, and the prairie style is best suited to medium-sized or large yards.

2 Repeated plants

The plantings by Dan Pearson at Home Farm, Northamptonshire, England, typify a naturalistic style. Grasses, including *Stipa tenuissima* and *Molinia caerulea*, and perennials, such as verbenas, sea hollies, and poppies, are repeated in what appear to be random groups, reflecting the way they would naturally self-seed. This wild look is tempered by an avenue of more formal-looking limes.

3 Natural meadow

The wildlife gardens at Sticky Wicket, Dorset, England, include this meadow, restored by owners Pam and Peter Lewis. Rich with indigenous flowers, it includes corky-fruited water-dropwort, with its frothy white blooms, meadow cranesbill, and buttercups. These are mixed with grasses, such as crested dogstail and sweet vernal, which gives hay its distinctive scent. In the summer, the meadow dances with butterflies—common blues, gatekeepers, and skippers are regular visitors. Not many of us have a meadow-sized yard, but it is possible to attract wildlife to a patch just 15 ft (5 m) square.

Cottage planting

For many people, cottage planting is the very essence of an English country garden. A profusion of color and scents is achieved by combining herbaceous perennials, shrubs, roses, fruits and vegetables, and native hedging. The secret of success is skillful planning. A cottage garden may appear to be a haphazard mix, but every element will have been thought through in minute detail.

When considering this style for your garden, remember that, although beautiful in summer, cottage gardens have little visual appeal in winter, since they don't include much strong structural or evergreen planting. And, unlike prairie styles, a lot of preparation is needed, since most of the flowering plants used in cottage designs are heavy feeders. An initial application of manure before planting and subsequent mulching, plus staking taller species such as delphiniums, and constant pruning make it very high maintenance.

The great charm of this style is that it embraces many different types of plants: lupins, gladioli, hostas, peonies, foxgloves, lavatera, rudbeckia, hollyhocks, catmint, lavender, and roses. You can even sneak in your own, seemingly inappropriate, favorites. You may also grow fruit and vegetables in the center of the ornamental action, or lay a lawn to act as a soothing foil to the brightly colored bouquets.

The style works best adjacent to houses built from natural materials, but is less suitable for tiny gardens where some year-round interest is needed. Blend house walls into the garden by covering them with plants, such as old roses or climbing hydrangeas, and thread clematis and honeysuckle through trees or over pergolas.

1 Fairy-tale planting

Snow-white roses draped over this rustic arch create instant nostalgia and romance. Like an illustration from a fairy-tale wedding, this is cottage garden planting at its best. You can almost smell the lavender wafting on a warm breeze.

2 Rich layers

Sleightholmedale in Yorkshire, England, boasts these superb cottage gardens. Adhering to Gertrude Jekyll's principles, the plants are laid out in loose drifts, and the soft color palette forms a harmonious and peaceful scene. Traditional cottage plants are employed to great effect, and include silver-leaved *Lychnis coronaria* 'Alba', astrantias, foxgloves, lilies, peonies, and roses tumbling over the pergola.

3 Blue accent

Traditional arbors make wonderful focal features for cottage gardens. This blue wooden seat at Wollerton Old Hall in Shropshire, England, marks the end of this section of the Rose Garden, and complements the style and colors of the burgeoning planting plan. Catmint frames the front of the picture, and tall spires of white rosebay willow herb (*Epilobium hirsutum* 'Album') create accents that help to define white, red and pink roses, and the magenta blooms of *Geranium psilostemon* on either side.

Modernist planting

There are many modern planting styles, but for the purists, a Modernist plan uses stark blocks of single species to create dramatic effects. The style also employs plants that suit the local site and situation, and designers attempt to link these with the surrounding landscapes. Colors can be subdued, maintenance tends to be minimal, and architectural topiary in spherical or box shapes provides structure and form. The style first came to prominence over 50 years ago, but it is now back in fashion, and you will see Modernist planting plans in many contemporary designs.

But, to some extent, you can interpret the term "modern" in any way you like. For example, contemporary planting may not be Modernist, but can simply be a new interpretation of more traditional styles. And over recent years, I have seen groups of grasses, Japanese-style planting, and architectural exotics all called "modern."

1

3

1 Beautiful blocks

The repeated plants and geometric shapes in this garden by Fiona Brockhoff demonstrate the graphic quality of a Modernist design. The Australian garden includes plants suited to the climate, such as the dryland tea tree (*Melaleuca lanceolata*), clipped into lollipop trees, and the tufty grass, *Stipa stipoides*. Silver-leaved *Leucophyta brownii* sparkles at the front of the planting group.

2 Reflections

The planting in this Dutch garden in Alphen aan Rijn typifies the Modernist style. Rectangular pools mirror the sky and water beyond the boundaries, and echo a slab-like bed of tall miscanthus.

3 Contemporary cool

This stunning modern home at Hope Ranch, California, demands a garden that allows its graphic beauty to shine, and the subtle design here does just that. A blanket of whipcord hebe (*H. cupressoides*) provides a backdrop to the flowers in front and contrasts with the vertical lines of the building. Swaths of purple *Erodium manescaui* and the daisylike *Erigeron karvinskianus* inject color and texture, while yellow kangaroo paw (*Anigozanthos pulcherrimus*) provides a vertical accent.

4 Urban chic

Clipped boxwood topiary, groups of white impatiens, and hostas and palms create a neat contemporary look in this small city garden by Belgians Claes and Humblet.

Container planting

Containers have always been popular because they allow people to grow plants that would normally be unsuitable for their climate or soil. Pots are also great fun; they have infinite uses and can create many exciting design effects.

Think about the shape and style of your pots, and try to envision your whole display as a complete unit. Getting the right balance of plants to containers is key, and may depend on the effect you wish to achieve. Do you want the pot to be the feature, or the plants? Try playing with sizes: small plants peeking out of the top of a large container can look quirky, but large, leafy specimens in small containers may look top-heavy. Experiment to see what works for you.

As a general rule, I find large pots more dramatic than small containers. They also require less maintenance, but can be heavy and difficult to move, so either plant them up *in situ*, or look for those made from lightweight materials.

Use containers to shape your garden style, too. Tall pots planted with, say, half-standard clipped bay trees, can help to define the entrance to an informal yard, or place four containers in each corner of a garden to confer formality. Pots also make beautiful focal points, or you can integrate them into an overall planting plan by sinking them into the borders. Alternatively, use pots and urns without planting as architectural features.

Food and drink Plants in pots cannot feed or drink from the ground, which means you have to supply everything they need. Ensure that the soil or compost and the amount of fertilizer and water you provide are right for your plants. Every spring, carefully replace the top few inches of growing medium with fresh material. And add a layer of gravel, decorative aggregates, or pebbles on top of the soil to help retain moisture.

1 Plants on wheels

These innovative planters were designed by Stephen Woodhams for a roof terrace in London. They are equipped with wheels that make them easy to move around the space. In winter, they can be wheeled to a sheltered spot where pruning and replanting can be carried out to minimize mess.

2 Beds and seats

Communal gardens must be low-maintenance, which is why I decided to use giant container-like raised beds for this newly planted garden. They elevate the soil level to a height that makes the plants easy to tend, and the retaining walls also double as seats.

3 Flowing pots

American designer Steve Martino has a great eye for graphic detail. These square, cast concrete containers flow gracefully down the flight of steps, while unruly stems of lady's slipper (*Pedilanthus macrocarpus*) explode out of them like fireworks.

4 Garden guards

Standing like sentries at the gateway to a small town garden, these oversized terracotta pots neatly topped with boxwood finials make a dramatic entrance. City gardens may be protected from frost, but in more exposed, colder areas, you should buy frostproof terracotta that has been fired to a high temperature. Frost-resistant terracotta means just that—it is resistant but may crack if temperatures plummet.

Structural plants

Carefully placed structural plants, such as trees and shrubs, create natural walls and dividers in the garden. Evergreens can be used as solid hedges to enclose an area or to provide year-round color and form in a border, while deciduous plants offer seasonal interest in the form of flowers, berries, and fall leaf color. Here is a small selection of my favorite architectural plants to whet your appetite.

1 Spotted laurel

Aucuba japonica 'Crotonifolia'
This tough evergreen grows in dry shade, withstands pollution and salt winds, and produces beautiful bright red fall berries.
Z 6–15   H 10 ft (3 m)   S 10 ft (3 m)

2 Erman's birch

Betula ermanii
Birches are happy in most sites and soils, and this one has pinkish or creamy-white bark and catkins.
Z 5–8   H 70 ft (20 m)   S 40 ft (12 m)

3 Golden hop

Humulus lupulus 'Aureus'
This twining climber, with hairy shoots and golden yellow leaves, grows best in sun or partial shade.
Z 4–8   H 20 ft (6 m)

4 Golden willow

Salix alba subsp. *vitellina* 'Britzensis'
Cut the stems of this willow to the ground in spring to encourage bright orange-red winter shoots.
Z 4–9   H 80 ft (25 m)   S 30 ft (10 m)

5 Oriental sweet gum

Liquidambar orientalis
Especially beautiful in fall, when the leaves turn yellow and orange, liquidambars do best in full sun.
Z 7–9   H 20 ft (6 m)   S 12 ft (4 m)

6 California lilac

Ceanothus 'Blue Mound'
A mound-forming evergreen with dark blue flowers in late spring.
Z 9–10   H 5 ft (1.5 m)   S 6 ft (2 m)

7 Skimmia
Skimmia japonica
Architectural and dome-shaped, this evergreen has white, scented spring flowers and red fall berries on female plants.
Z 7–9   H 20 ft (6 m)   S 20 ft (6 m)

8 Smoke bush
Cotinus coggygria Purpureus Group
The smoke bush has fluffy fruiting panicles in summer, and its leaves turn orange and red in fall.
Z 5–9   H 15 ft (5 m)   S 15 ft (5 m)

9 Lavender
Lavandula angustifolia 'Munstead'
This wonderful lavender has long spikes of fragrant blue-purple flowers from mid- to late summer.
Z 5–8   H 18 in (45 cm)   S 24 in (60 cm)

10 Boston ivy
Parthenocissus tricuspidata
A vigorous deciduous climber, its bright green leaves turn brilliant red to purple in fall.
Z 4–8   H 70 ft (20 m)

11 Milkweed
Euphorbia characias subsp. *wulfenii*
Whatever the site, there is always a euphorbia to suit. This tall species has architectural stems with blue leaves and yellow flowerheads.
Z 7–11   H 4 ft (1.2 m)   S 4 ft (1.2 m)

12 Japanese maple
Acer palmatum
There are many forms of Japanese maples, but all have decorative foliage and produce a vibrant show of color in the fall.
Z 5–8   H 25 ft (8 m)   S 30 ft (10 m)

Also consider
Buxus sempervirens 'Suffruticosa';
Carpinus betulus 'Fastigiata';
Photinia x *fraseri* 'Red Robin';
Prunus serrula; *Rosmarinus officinalis*; *Taxus baccata*.

Focal plants

With eye-catching bark, leaves, flowers, fruits, or berries, focal plants can have strong form, and create striking shapes. Some plants only shine for a moment, others for a whole season, but whatever their particular talents, they always provide visual highlights in a garden. Use them in containers at the end of a pathway, in a gravel bed to strike a pose, or to provide focus and excitement in a border.

1 Yoshino cherry

Prunus x yedoensis
Delicate bowls of pale pink blossoms, which fade to white, cover arching branches in early spring.
Z 5–8 H 50 ft (15 m) S 30 ft (10 m)

2 Agave

Agave parryi
The rosette of thick blue leaves is set off by stems of pink or red buds and creamy-yellow summer flowers.
Z 9–11 H 20 in (50 cm)
S to 3 ft (1 m)

3 Woolly tree fern

Dicksonia antarctica
The tree fern has been around since prehistoric times, yet it is perfect for a contemporary look.
Z 12–15 H to 20 ft (6 m)
S 12 ft (4 m)

4 Japanese banana

Musa basjoo
This banana plant's fruit tastes terrible, but it's worth growing for its structural paddle-shaped leaves.
Z 8–11 H 15 ft (5 m)
S 12 ft (4 m)

5 Agave

Agave geminiflora
This agave has a dynamic quality with its slender, spiky leaves.
Z 9–11 H 24 in (60 cm)
S 24 in (60 cm)

6 Crabapple

Malus tschonoskii
This tree's fiery fall foliage is matched by yellow red-flushed fruit.
Z 5–8 H 40 ft (12 m) S 22 ft (7 m)

7 Phormium
Phormium 'Sundowner'
The long, lance-shaped leaves of
phormiums seem to explode out
of the ground. 'Sundowner' has
pretty, dark rose-pink edges.
Z 9–11   H 6 ft (2 m)
S 6 ft (2 m)

8 Honey bush
Melianthus major
Particularly useful in coastal
gardens, the honey bush is a
slightly tender spreading shrub.
Deep brick-red flowers appear
from late spring to midsummer.
Z 8–11   H 6–10 ft (2–3 m)
S 3–10 ft (1–3 m)

9 Canna
Canna 'Durban'
Grown for their large, dramatic
leaves, cannas also sport brightly
colored flowers in late summer.
'Durban' is particularly stunning
with red- and yellow-striped leaves.
Z 8–11   H 5 ft (1.5 m)
S 24 in (60 cm)

10 Foxtail lily
Eremurus stenophyllus subsp.
stenophyllus
Great conical spikes of brilliant
yellow flowers shoot up from early
to midsummer from a rosette of
gray-green leaves.
Z 5–8   H to 5 ft (1.5 m)
S 30 in (75 cm)

11 Castor oil plant
Ricinus communis 'Gibsonii'
Everything about this plant is
dramatic. Its brilliant pink flowers,
red stems, and dark purple leaves
together scream, "Look at me!"
Z 11–14   H 6 ft (1.8 m)
S 3–4 ft (1–1.2 m)

Also consider
Acer palmatum 'Garnet'; *Corylus
avellana* 'Contorta'; *Echium
wildpretii*; *Ensete ventricosum*;
Fatsia japonica 'Variegata'.

Filler plants

Use herbaceous perennials, annuals, and bulbs to color in the gaps between structural and focal plants, and to provide seasonal interest throughout the year. Mix your palette of colors and textures for a romantic look, or limit the tones for an elegant, formal design. Plant in bold swaths, and avoid dotting your beds with one or two plants here and there, which can look messy and unsatisfying.

1 Milkweed
Euphorbia polychroma
Offers long-lasting flower heads from midspring to midsummer.
Z 5–9 H 16 in (40 cm)
S 24 in (60 cm)

2 Gayfeather
Liatris spicata 'Kobold'
Spikes of wacky, fluffy flowers emerge from grasslike foliage.
Z 4–9 H to 20 in (50 cm)
S 18 in (45 cm)

3 Red-hot poker
Kniphofia caulescens
The coral-red flowers of this red hot poker fade to pale yellow and are slightly more subdued than those of its vibrant relatives.
Z 6–9 H 4 ft (1.2 m) S 24 in (60 cm)

4 Foxglove
Digitalis purpurea f. *albiflora*
Foxgloves tower out of shady borders, their long stems adorned with pretty cup-shaped flowers.
Z 5–9 H 3–6 ft (1–2 m)
S to 24 in (60 cm)

5 Geranium
Geranium x *magnificum*
Masses of dark-veined, rich violet flowers cover this superb plant.
Z 4–8 H 24 in (60 cm)
S 24 in (60 cm)

6 Hattie's pincushion
Astrantia 'Hadspen Blood'
Dark red bracts and flowers stand out above deeply divided leaves.
Z 4–7 H 12–36 in (30–90 cm)
S 18 in (45 cm)

7 Santolina
Santolina rosmarinifolia subsp. *rosmarinifolia*
The creamy-yellow button flowers emerge in summer out of dark evergreen scented foliage.
Z 6–9   H 24 in (60 cm)
S 3 ft (1 m)

8 Soft shield fern
Polystichum setiferum
The dark green fronds of this fern provide a textured blanket in a shady area of the garden.
Z 6–9   H 4 ft (1.2 m)
S 36 in (90 cm)

9 Plantain lily
Hosta fortunei var. *aureomarginata*
Deeply veined, heart-shaped, olive-green leaves with creamy margins are accompanied by tall spikes of mauve flowers in summer.
Z 3–9   H 22 in (55 cm)   S 3 ft (1 m)

10 Japanese anemone
Anemone x *hybrida* 'Luise Uhink'
A vigorous Japanese anemone with wonderful, large, semi-double white flowers. Prefers partial shade.
Z 4–8   H 4–5 ft (1.2–1.5 m)
S indefinite

11 Tulip
Tulipa 'Pink Impression'
Plant these rose-flushed tulips close to flowering perennials that will take the stage as the tulips fade.
Z 3–8   H 22 in (55 cm)

12 Ornamental onion
Allium aflatunense
Purple-pink pompom flower heads stand on tall straight stems like giant lollipops.
Z 4–8   H 3 ft (1 m)   S 4 in (10 cm)

Also consider
Aconitum carmichaelii 'Arendsii'; *Crocosmia* 'Lucifer'; *Echinacea purpurea* 'Robert Bloom'; *Nigella damascena* Persian Jewel Series; *Verbascum chaixii* 'Album'.

Grasses and bamboos

Bamboos and grasses work on many different levels. Loose informal grasses dance and rustle in the breeze, injecting borders with sound and movement, while sturdy, tufty types provide structure and form, either as focals in a pot or *en masse* in a modern planting plan. Bamboo canes provide vertical accents, and add color and height to gravel beds, containers, or themed Asian and Zen gardens.

1 Fountain grass
Pennisetum alopecuroides 'Hameln'
The flowers of this billowing grass resemble gray-white cats' tails. The leaves turn gold in fall.
Z 6–9   H 2–5 ft (0.6–1.5 m)
S 2–4 ft (0.6–1.2 m)

2 Fountain bamboo
Fargesia nitida
One of the few slow-growing bamboos, with dark purple-green canes that are lined purple-brown.
Z 5–9   H to 15 ft (5 m)
S 5 ft (1.5 m)

3 Pampas grass
Cortaderia selloana
Dense tufts of arching, glaucous leaves are set off in late summer by silky silver plumes on tall stems.
Z 7–11   H 8–10 ft (2.5–3 m)
S 5 ft (1.5 m)

4 Giant feather grass
Stipa gigantea
The silvery, purple-green spikelets of this tall grass ripen to gold.
Z 8–15   H to 8 ft (2.5 m)   S 4 ft (1.2 m)

5 Gardeners' garters
Phalaris arundinacea var. *picta*
Gardeners' garters has decorative white-striped leaves and white to pale pink flowers, but be warned: it is rampant and spreads like fury.
Z 4–9   H to 3 ft (1 m)   S indefinite

6 Sasa
Sasa quelpaertensis
The spectacular large leaves of this bamboo make good groundcover.
Z 7–11   H 32 in (80 cm)   S indefinite

7 Japanese blood grass

Imperata cylindrica 'Rubra'
Slow-spreading grass with flat
lime-green leaves that rapidly turn
a stunning blood-red from the tips
down to the bases.
z 5–9   h 16 in (40 cm)
s 12 in (30 cm) or more

8 Miscanthus

Miscanthus sinensis 'Malepartus'
Elegant wine-red flower plumes
appear among the white striped
leaves in summer, and the whole
plant then turns yellow in fall.
z 5–9   h 6 ft (1.8 m) s 4 ft (1.2 m)

9 Bowles' golden sedge

Carex elata 'Aurea'
Dense clumps of arching yellow
leaves with narrow green margins.
z 5–9   h to 28 in (70 cm)
s 18 in (45 cm)

10 Black lilyturf

Ophiopogon planiscapus
'Nigrescens'
With its signature curving, black
leaves, this grasslike plant also
sports pale pink summer flowers
followed by shiny black berries.
z 6–11 h 8 in (20 cm) s 8 in (20 cm)

11 Blue fescue

Festuca glauca 'Elijah Blue'
In summer, this fescue grass bears
violet-flushed flowers above its
dense tufts of blue-green leaves.
z 4–8   h to 12 in (30 cm)
s 10 in (25 cm)

12 Maiden grass

Miscanthus sinensis 'Gracillimus'
The very narrow curved leaves
with white midribs turn a lovely
bronze color in the fall.
z 5–9   h 4½ ft (1.3 m) s 4 ft (1.2 m)

Also consider

Hakonechloa macra; *Melica
altissima* 'Atropurpurea';
Pleioblastus pygmaeus;
Phyllostachys aurea.

183

Water and bog plants

Introduce water to your garden for its magical qualities and the opportunity to grow a new range of plants. Choose from: bog plants that thrive in moist soil at the edges of natural ponds; marginals, which prefer shallow water; floaters, such as water lilies, whose leaves and flowers float on the surface; submerged aquatics that live below the water line; and oxygenators that help to keep the water clear.

1 Kingcup
Caltha palustris
A marginal or bog plant, kingcup bears waxy yellow spring flowers.
Z 3–7   H 4–16 in (10–40 cm)
S 18 in (45 cm)

2 Primula
Primula vialii
Grow this primula in damp soil for its brilliant crimson and pink cone-shaped summer flowers.
Z 5–8   H 12–24 in (30–60 cm)
S 12 in (30 cm)

3 Golden arum
Zantedeschia elliottiana
The elegant heart-shaped leaves and waxy trumpet-shaped flowers make this a bog-garden favorite.
Z 8–10   H 24–36 in (60–90 cm)
S 8 in (20 cm)

4 Gunnera
Gunnera manicata
Huge palmate leaves and unusual flower heads create structure and form in a bog garden.
Z 7–11   H 8 ft (2.5 m)   S 10–12 ft (3–4 m)

5 Japanese water iris
Iris laevigata
This marginal has straplike leaves and purple-blue summer flowers.
Z 4–9   H 32 in (80 cm)   S 12 in (30 cm)

6 Yellow flag
Iris pseudacorus
This iris thrives in pond margins and has flowers with yellow petals with brown or violet markings.
Z 5–8   H 3–5 ft (0.9–1.5 m)

7 Water lily
Nymphaea tetragona
Perfect for small pools, this little
water lily bears fragrant white
blooms from summer to fall.
Z 3–11   S 10–16 in (25–40 cm)

8 Water lily
Nymphaea 'James Brydon'
The rounded bronze-green leaves
show off the rich pink flowers.
Z 3–11   S 3–4 ft (0.9–1.2 m)

9 Globeflower
Trollius x *cultorum* 'Alabaster'
Less vigorous than most cultivars,
this pretty bog plant bears pale
yellow flowers in mid- to late spring.
Z 5–8   H to 24 in (60 cm)   S to 16 in
(40 cm)

10 Cattail
Typha latifolia
With their long strap-shaped leaves
and dark brown flower spikes,
cattails are striking marginals.
Z 2–11   H 6 ft (2 m)   S indefinite

11 Water lettuce
Pistia stratiotes
With evergreen leaves like little
ribbed fans, water lettuce is a
floater for a warm sheltered pond.
Z 9–11   H 4 in (10 cm)
S indefinite

12 Pickerel weed
Pontederia cordata
A lovely marginal with spikes of
tubular blue flowers in late summer,
and spear-shaped foliage.
Z 3–11   H 3–4½ ft (0.9–1.3 m)
S 24–30 in (60–75 cm)

Also consider
*Cyperus papyrus; Lobelia
cardinalis; Mentha aquatica;
Rheum palmatum.*

Oxygenating plants
*Ceratophyllum demersum;
Lagarosiphon major;
Potamogeton crispus.*

10

DESIGNING WITH PLANTS **WATER AND BOG PLANTS**

185

Index

Photo credits

The publisher would like to thank the following for their kind permission to reproduce their photographs:

Abbreviations key: **t**=top, **b**=bottom, **r**=right, **l**=left, **c**=centre

2 Jane Sebire/Design:James Hitchmough & Amanda Stokes 7 Henk Dijkman/Design: Jan Nickman, "Puur", Holland 12(t) Clive Nichols/Design: Wynniatt-Husey Clarke, (b) Jerry Harpur/Design: Oehme & van Sweden Associates, USA 13(tl) Clive Nichols/Design: Ilga Jansons & Mike Dryfoos, Seattle, USA, (tr) Helen Fickling/Raymond Jungles Inc. Florida, (b) Liz Eddison/Design: Nicholas J Boult, Tatton Park 2002 14(tl) Corbis, (tr) Marianne Majerus Photography, (b) Clive Nichols/Rosemary Pearson 15(t) Garden Picture Library/Steve Wooster/Design: Ted Smyth, New Zealand, (bl) Jerry Harpur/Design: Jamie Durie, NSW, Australia, (br) Nicola Browne/Design: Topher Delaney, San Francisco 16(t) Andrew Lawson/Design: Caroline Burgess, Stonecrop, USA, (bl) Jerry Harpur/Design: Naila Green, Dawlish, Devon, (br) Marijke Heuff/House Bingergen, Angerlo, Holland 17(t) Modeste Herwig/Marston & Langinger Ltd, Chelsea Flower Show, (b) DK/Peter Anderson 18(t) Clive Nichols/Design: Ilga Jansons & Mike Dryfoos, Seattle, USA, (tr) Jonathan Buckley/Design: Diarmuid Gavin, (br) Mark Bolton/Mythic Garden, Stone Lane Gardens, Devon 19(b) Marijke Heuff/Design: Loekie Schwartz, Holland, (t) Juliette Wade/Mr & Mrs JH Benyon, Bleak House, Bagnall, Staffordshire 23(tl) Tim Street-Porter/Design: Luis Barragán, (tc) Jonathan Buckley/Design: Diarmuid Gavin, (tr) Andrew Lawson/Design: Hardy Amis, & (c) Wollerton Old Hall, Shrops, (cl & cr) Helen Fickling/Design: Raymond Jungles Inc. Florida, (bl) Photonica/Laura Hanifin, (bc) Jerry Harpur/Design: Luciano Giubbilei, London, & (br) Design: Simon Fraser, Hampton, Middx 24 Helen Fickling/Design: Andy Sturgeon & Stephen Reilly, Westonbirt Festival of the Garden 2003 25(t) Henk Dijkman/Design: Paul Weijers, Garden Essentials, Haarlem, Holland, (b) Marion Brenner/Design: Andrea Cochran Landscape Architecture 26(t) Nicola Browne/Design: Jinny Blom, London, (b) Henk Dijkman/Design: Jan Nickman, "Puur", Holland 27(t) Gil Hanly/Ron Sang, Auckland/Design: Ted Smyth, New Zealand, (b) Tim Street-Porter/Design: Luis Barragán 28(t) Andrew Lawson/Design: Kathy Brown, (b) Le Scanff-Mayer/Gamberaia, Tuscany 29 John Glover/Camden Hill Sq, London 30(t) Jonathan Buckley/Design: Diarmuid Gavin, (b) Jerry Harpur/The Marchioness of Salisbury, Hatfield House, Herts 31(t) Jane Sebire/Design: Frank & Marjorie Lawley, Herterton House, Northumberland, (b) Andrew Lawson/Wollerton Old Hall, Shrops, 32 DK/Jacqui Hurst 33 Andrew Lawson/Design: Hardy Amis 34(t) S & O Mathews Photography, (b) Rex Features 35(t) DK/Angus Beare, (b) Jerry Harpur/Sleightholmedale Lodge, Yorks 36(t) Steve Gunther/Patrick Mahoney, Anaheim, CA, USA, (b) Marcus Harpur/Design: Paul Spraklin, South Benfleet, Essex 37(t) Jerry Harpur/Design: Made Wijaya, Bali, (b) Helen Fickling/Design: Raymond Jungles Inc. Florida 38(t) Jane Sebire/Design: Frank & Marjorie Lawley, Herterton House, Northumberland (t) S & O Mathews Photography/Briar Rose Cottage, Orinoco, New Zealand, (b) Andrew Lawson/Wollerton Old Hall, Shrops 39 (tl) Liz Eddison/Design: Mr & Mrs Ottey, (tr) Marianne Majerus Photography/Design: Johan Heirman, (b) DK/Steve Wooster 40(t) Alamy Images/Arcaid, (b) Garden Picture Library/John Glover/Design: Hiroshi Nanmori, Chelsea Flower Show 1996 41(t) Andrew Lawson/Jojakko-Ji, Kyoto, Japan, (b) Gil Hanly/Ron Sang garden/Design: Ted Smyth, New Zealand 42(l) Marianne Majerus Photography/Design: Helen Pitel, (r) Marijke Heuff/House Bingerden, Angerlo, Holland 43(t) Alamy Images/John James, (b) Andrew Lawson/Rofford Manor/Design: Michael Balston 44(l) Nicola Browne/Design: Ted Smyth, New Zealand, (r) Jerry Harpur/Design: Steve Martino, Arizona, USA 45(b) Helen Fickling/Design: Raymond Jungles Inc. Florida, (t) Garden Picture Library/Ron Sutherland/Design: Anthony Paul 46(l) Rex Features, (r) Photonica/Laura Hanifin 47(tl) Tony Heywood's Conceptual Gardens, (tr) Alamy Images/Yuri Lev, (b) Andrew Lawson/Design: Ivan Hicks 48(t) Jerry Harpur/Design: Luciano Giubbilei, London, (b) Marianne Majerus Photography/Sculptures by Joanna Mowbray and Bruno Romeda 49(t) Musee Albert-Kahn/Departement des Hauts-de-Seine/Philippe Planchon/Artist: Takano Fumiako, (b) Photonica/Charles Gullung 50 Marianne Majerus Photography 51(tl) Jerry Harpur/Design: Simon Fraser, Hampton, Middx, (r) Rex Features, (b) Marianne Majerus Photography/Design: Jill Billington & Mimi Harris 55(tr) John Glover/Carl St, San Francisco/Design: Chris Jacobsen, (tl) John Glover/Design: Fiona Lawrenson, (bl) Jerry Harpur/Design: John Bailey, London, (br) Andrew Lawson/Design: Helen Dillon, Dublin 58-59 Andrew Lawson/Design: Camilla Shivarg 60-61 John Glover/Design: Fiona Lawrenson 62-63 John Glover/Carl St, San Francisco/Design Chris Jacobsen 64-65 Andrew Lawson/Design: Helen Dillon, Dublin 66-67 Concept for Living Ltd 68-69 Jerry Harpur/Design: John Bailey, London 73(tl) Marianne Majerus Photography/Design: Susanne Blair & (bl) Design: Katherine Swift, (tr) Andrew Lawson/Design: Penelope Hobhouse, (br) Liz Eddison/Design: Nic Horsey 74(l) John Glover/Design: Pamela Woods, (r) Garden Picture Library/John Miller 75(l) Alamy Images/Garden Picture Library, (r) John Glover 76(l) Marianne Majerus Photography/Design: Susanne Blair, (r) Marion Brenner/Design:Andrea Cochrane Landscape Architecture 77(l) Marianne Majerus Photography/Design: Susanne Blair, (r) Jonathan Buckley/ Design: Diarmuid Gavin 78 John Glover/Design: Helen Dillon, Dublin 80 Marianne Majerus/Design: Dominique Lubar 81 Marianne Majerus Photography/Design: Joe Swift 82 Marianne Majerus Photography/Sir Mark and Lady Potter 84 Marianne Majerus Photography/Design: John Mixer 86 Nicola Browne/Design: Ross Palmer 93 Garden Picture Library/Nigel Francis 94 Alamy Images/Stock Connection Inc 95 Garden Picture Library/Clive Nichols 96-97 Garden Picture Library/John Glover 98 Garden Picture Library/Jane Legate 99 Garden Picture Library/Eric Crichton 100 Jerry Harpur/Design: Gunilla Pickard, Essex 101 Marcus Harpur/Dennis Neate 102 Mel Watson 105 (2nd row (l) & (4th row (c)) Marianne Majerus Photography, (2nd row r) DK/Cyril Laubscher 106 Garden Picture Library/Mark Bolton 108(t) Holt Studios/Primrose Peacock, (b) A-Z Botanical Collection/Geoff Kidd/RHS Rosemoor, Devon 109(l) Garden Picture Library/Henk Dijkman/Design: Henk Weijers, Holland, (r) Sunniva Harte 110-111 DK/Peter Anderson 121(bl) Jonathan Buckley/Design: Diarmuid Gavin 128 www.factoryfurniture.co.uk 131(tl) Jo Whitworth/Design: Christina and Nigel Oates, Fovant Hut Garden, Salisbury, Wilts. Open to public. Tel: 01722 714756,

Diarmuid thanks...

To my co-writer and my partner in life, Justine Keane.

The creation of this book has been very much a team effort. Its genesis was creative, but also turbulent. It was wonderful to work with such a strong team at DK.

David Lamb has always been the godfather, the guiding light. A pint of Guinness in Dublin is in order I think.

Zia Allaway held on steady through the fast and the furious, and steered the project into calm waters. A superb editor – thank you, Zia.

Colin Walton worried for this book, but put his everything into ensuring it lived up to his exacting design standards and dragged me along with him. Thank you.

Mel Watson for her wonderfully enthusiastic Sherlock Holmes-like picture research.

Richard Lee for his superb illustrations.

Vicky Willan for her dedication and research. Anna Kruger and Christine Dyer for overseeing the words.

Peter Luff and Lee Griffiths for their design input; and Louise Waller for DTP.

Hermione Ireland and the rest at DK Publicity and Marketing for a memorable party atop the Strand.

And DK New York: Chuck Lang, Jessica Miller, Therese Burke, Jeanie Guman, Connie Carson, and Cathy Melnicki.

At John Noel Management, thanks to Katherine, John, Nik, Polly, Brian, Katy, Dee, and Louise.

A special thanks to Mark Robinson at Diarmuid Gavin Designs – thanks for keeping the show on the road; Laurence Keilty for making the designs look so good, and Neil Gavin for the inspired photography.

All the gardeners and designers whose work is featured. This is a book about our wonderful profession. Some of you I know, but thanks to you all for your creative gardens.

And all the photographers who bring our gardens to a wide audience. Thank you for your dedication.

Those at the BBC who've been my patrons for many years: thank you to Jane Root, Tom Archer, Rachel Innes-Lumsden, Dan Adamson, Hannah Weston, Basil Comely, and Matthew Thompson.

At Chelsea 2004, thanks to: Denise and Will Dean, Sean and Paul Cunningham, Annette Dalton, Gary Graham from Bord Glas (Irish Horticultural Board), Steve Poole, Robert Letts, Claire Martin, Julian Mercer, Steve Greenwood, Mike Lax and Eva Cieszewska, Andrew and Margi from Tendercare, Vince Matthews and Stephen Preece at Marshalls, Laurence and Alice Dallaglio, Stuart Higgins, Jackie Wilson at the National Lottery, Anita Collins, Mary Reynolds, Valerie Beck, Laurence and Jackie Lewellyn-Bowen, Jason and Dean at Factory Furniture, Warwick and Sally, Microsoft, the Curious Gardeners, Alan Titchmarsh, Charlie Dimmock, Catherine and Jim, and all at HG Wells and Sons, Isle of Wight.

Tom and Jackie Gallagher, Matt, and everyone at Elite Metalcraft, thanks for the continual commitment to creating something different.

The McDevitts at the Newlands Garden Centre, Clondalkin, Dublin 5.

Jack and Joan Gavin, Declan, Niamh, Emer, Susan, Gerry, David, Rebecca, Jack, Ella and Hannah. Terry and Ronan Keane, Madeleine, Tim, Jane, Karl, Natasha, Julia, Holly and Ben.

The Byrnes in Billericay, the Mannings in Liverpool, Karen and Sally at Jaguar, Paul Martin and Steve Davis at AIB, Jay, Tony, Richard, Branton, Jason and Sam, George Copalis, Jay and Ann, Kay Godleman, Amanda and Simon Ross, Neil Gavin, Robin Matthews, Monie Begley, George Dunnington, Dave Smith, and David Symonds.